CARIBBEAN
Flavors

For Adara

CARIBBEAN
Flavors

Wendy Rahamut

*Over 150 recipes from
the heart of the Caribbean*

MACMILLAN
CARIBBEAN

Macmillan Education
Between Towns Road, Oxford OX4 3PP
A division of Macmillan Publishers Limited
Companies and representatives throughout the world

www.macmillan-caribbean.com

ISBN 978-1-4050-2737-3

Text © Wendy Rahamut 2002
Photographs © Aldwyn Sin Pang 2002
Design and illustration © Macmillan Publishers Limited 2002

First published 2002

Designed by Linda Reed & Associates
Cover design by Gary Fielder, AC Design
Photograph of author by Michael Bonaparte
Food styling by Wendy Rahamut
Index compiled by Valerie Chandler

Printed in Malaysia

2011   2010   2009   2008
14   13   12   11   10   9   8   7

Contents

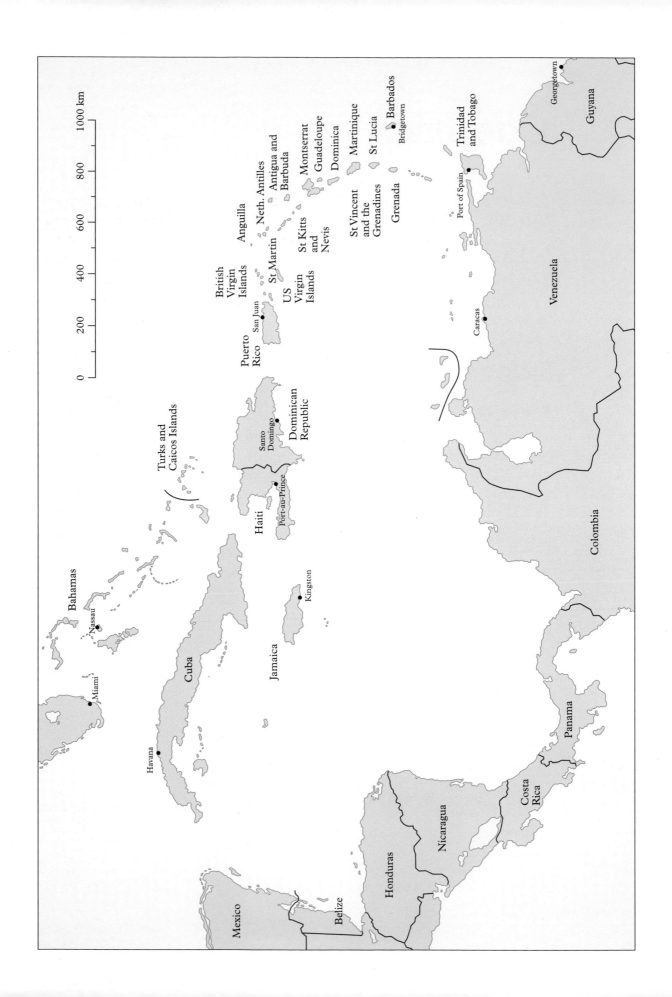

Introduction

Located in the Caribbean Sea between North and South America, from Cuba to Trinidad and Tobago, the Caribbean islands boast influences from the East Indians, Africans, Chinese, South Americans, North Americans, the English and Europeans, South East Asians and the Syrian Lebanese. The foods of our islands represent an intermingling of cultures giving way to a cuisine that is mouthwatering, spicy and delicious!

Each of these cultures has made an indigenous mark on the foods of the region, truly reflecting a type of fusion cuisine of the Caribbean indeed. This is what *Caribbean Flavors* is about – not only can you find true indigenous foods of this region in this book, but you will experience a new type of Caribbean fusion cooking that is coming out of these islands today: a fresher and brighter twist, resulting in a spicy and exciting style of cooking.

The delicious flavors of our sunkissed islands are reflected by the spicy hot curries and rotis of the East Indians; the stews, dumplings, ground provisions and rice and peas cookups from the African influences. The Chinese have become a mainstay with their localized versions of traditional favorites, such as fried rice, noodle cakes, stuffed dumplings and meat and shrimp stirfries. The Europeans and English have left their mark as seen through our varied desserts, ice creams and pastries; the Americans their barbecues. The South and Central Americans have given us the gift of cornmeal-inspired dishes like arepas and pastelles; and the Syrian Lebanese have given us delicious salads, roasted meat kebabs and kibbehs, to name a few.

All these influences have given birth to a new cuisine that is infused with our locally grown herbs and spices and fired up to perfection with our variety of hot peppers.

And don't forget the lusciousness of Caribbean fruits! Juicy-fleshed mangoes, sunset paw paws, sugary sweet pineapples, tender smooth bananas and figs, perfumed passion fruits, fresh coconuts. These have shown the way to new and exciting desserts and other sweet treats.

This is the cooking of the Caribbean today, a cuisine to make your mouth water and have your tastebuds jump for joy!

Go ahead and enjoy a taste of our islands today!

WENDY RAHAMUT

Conversion tables

Weights

1 ounce	30 grams
8 ounces or ½ pound	250 grams or ¼ kilogram
16 ounces or 1 pound	500 grams or ½ kilogram
32 ounces or 2 pounds	1000 grams or 1 kilogram

Volumes

1 teaspoon	5 ml
1 tablespoon	15 ml
½ cup	125 ml
1 cup	250 ml or ½ pint
2 cups	500 ml or 1 pint

Oven temperatures

250°F = 120°C
300°F = 150°C
350°F = 180°C
400°F = 200°C
450°F = 230°C
500°F = 260°C

Appetizer flavors

Cooking and eating in the Caribbean are very informal, with guests or friends often gathering to chat and spend time together or, as they call it in some parts, to 'lime'. There need not be a reason for a 'lime', it is just the pastime of many to get together, share a few drinks and have a good time. Food plays a very important part in socializing here and some type of food is always included in any gathering.

Drinks are always accompanied by small snacks, or finger foods, much like the tapas of Spain. These are called 'cutters' – spicy finger foods that accompany any drink, be it alcohol or non-alcohol. These cutters may be just a part of a casual get-together or they may be the appetizer before a meal. Because dining is informal here, many parties or gatherings do not serve meals in courses as a more formal environment may warrant. As a result the cutters may be passed around before the meal is served.

Fritters and pies are the most popular appetizers in the Caribbean. From Cuba through to Guyana the theme of these appetizers is hot and spicy, redolent with the flavors of dried spices and fresh herbs. Many are flavored with hot peppers and accompanied by some sort of hot and spicy salsa or chutney. Local produce always contributes to these delicious treats.

Plantains and cornmeal are used in many Spanish Caribbean islands to make enticing appetizers, such as plantain chips, pastelles and arepas. Avocados are used when in season throughout the islands. The French Caribbean country of Martinique loves to pair avocados with crabmeat and hot pepper. My version uses shrimp and serves the avocado and shrimp on pounded and fried plantains. Avocados are also used in spicy salsa and guacamole. Callaloo is a popular vegetable and is quite versatile as well. Its creamy consistency and mouthwatering goodness shine through when folded into a crepe or filled into a dough pocket for a delightful treat!

Indian delicacies from Trinidad and Tobago, such as seasoned potato pies and vegetable fritters made with split pea flour, all accompanied by a hot chutney, are favorites of these islands, and have become a familar street food as well. Jamaicans pride themselves on their beef patties – a spicy beef filling encased with a flaky pastry. My version uses a cornmeal dough with the spicy filling. The Syrian Lebanese have left their mark, as hummos (chickpea dip) is quite popular here as well, while the Chinese influence is seen in the popularity of filled dumplings and spring rolls!

The recipes that follow marry a bit of the traditional and a bit of the new island cuisine to create exciting and mouthwatering delights.

Tropical spring rolls with tamarind plum sauce

These spring rolls are best served warm.

6 tbs cornstarch

½ cup water

vegetable oil

1 tbs chopped garlic

1 tbs minced ginger

¼ cup minced shrimp

2 cups finely shredded cabbage

2 carrots, shredded

4 Chinese dried black mushrooms, reconstituted, caps removed and chopped

1 tsp salt

1 tsp freshly ground black pepper

1 tbs sugar

4 blades fresh chive, finely chopped

2 tbs chopped chadon beni (cilantro)

25 spring roll wrappers or 50 wonton skins

◆ Combine the cornstarch with the water and set aside.

◆ Heat a clean wok, add 1 tablespoon oil, and when hot add the garlic and ginger. Add shrimp and stir and fry for 2 minutes. Add the cabbage, carrots and mushrooms and stir and fry until well blended. Season with the salt and pepper, and sprinkle on the sugar.

◆ Remove from heat and sprinkle on the herbs. Cool.

◆ Place wrapper so that one edge is pointing to you. Put about 1 tablespoon of filling in the center of the wrapper and spread to make a log. Fold the lower part up to cover filling, fold again, fold in the two sides, and continue folding to make a cylinder. Seal with the flour paste. Continue until all the wrappers are used.

◆ Deep fry spring rolls until golden brown, and serve with plum sauce.

Makes 25 large or 50 small

Tamarind plum sauce

½ cup Chinese plum sauce

2 tbs white vinegar

1 tbs tamarind sauce

1 tbs chopped chadon beni (cilantro)

2 cloves garlic, minced

1 tsp sugar

½ tsp seeded and chopped hot pepper

◆ Combine all the ingredients and refrigerate until ready for use.

Makes about ⅔ cup

Appetizers

Crabcakes with chili-lime mayonnaise

For the chili-lime mayonnaise

1 cup mayonnaise

1 cup natural yogurt

1 red bell pepper, roasted, seeded and puréed

1 tsp pepper sauce

2 cloves garlic, minced

1 tbs freshly squeezed lime juice

1½ tsp chili powder

2 tbs chopped chadon beni (cilantro)

2 tbs finely chopped chives

For the crabcakes

vegetable oil

2 onions, finely chopped

1 lb crabmeat

1 tbs Dijon mustard

1 tsp hot pepper sauce

2 cloves garlic, minced

½ tsp salt

1 tsp freshly ground black pepper

2 pimento peppers, seeded and minced

½ cup chopped chives

2 tbs thyme

2 tbs chopped celery

1 tbs lime juice

1½ cups fresh breadcrumbs

1 egg

◆ Make the mayonnaise by combining all the ingredients. Refrigerate until ready for use.

◆ Make the crabcakes. Heat 1 tablespoon vegetable oil in a skillet, and sauté the onions for about 5 minutes. Place in a large mixing bowl and add all the other ingredients. Mix well. The mixture should hold together, if it seems too crumbly, add a little water to bring it together.

◆ Shape mixture into 16–20 patties.

◆ Heat oil in skillet, and fry patties for about 3 minutes per side until golden brown.

◆ Drain and serve with the chili-lime mayonnaise.

Makes 16–20

Melt-in-your-mouth phoulorie

These are delicious fritters made with puréed and seasoned split peas. Serve with tamarind-mint chutney or mango chutney.

1 lb split peas

2 cloves garlic, minced

1 tsp saffron powder

¼ tsp baking soda

2 tsp baking powder

2 tbs flour

1½ tsp salt

1 tsp pepper sauce

vegetable oil for frying

◆ Wash the split peas, place in a bowl and cover with water. Leave to soak overnight.

◆ The next day, drain the split peas and grind in a food processor or food mill until the consistency is smooth.

◆ Add the garlic, saffron powder, baking soda, baking powder, flour, salt and pepper sauce. Allow to rest for 1 hour.

◆ If the mixture seems too dry add a little water. Beat with a wooden spoon to incorporate air and lighten the mixture.

◆ Heat oil in a deep fryer, and drop the mixture by teaspoons into the hot oil. Fry until golden brown or until the phoulorie float to the top of the oil.

◆ Drain and serve immediately.

Makes about 6 dozen

Baiganee

EGGPLANT AND SPLIT PEA FRITTERS

1 quantity phoulorie mixture

salt

1 eggplant, cut into ½ inch slices

vegetable oil for frying

◆ Salt the eggplant slices and let stand for 15 minutes. Then rinse and pat dry.

◆ Heat oil in a wok or deep skillet.

◆ Using your fingers or a small knife carefully paste the phoulorie mixture onto both sides of the eggplant slices and fry immediately until golden brown. Drain and serve with tamarind-mint chutney or mango chutney (see page 194).

Makes 12–15

Appetizers

Indian delicacies: Baiganee (front), Melt-in-your-mouth phoulorie (center), Quick saheena (back, page 6)

Appetizers

Appetizers

Quick saheena

SPINACH AND SPLIT PEA FRITTERS

These are delicious East Indian delicacies native to Trinidad made from ground split peas mixed with dasheen/callaloo leaves, but you may use spinach instead.

1 quantity phoulorie mixture

1 bunch young fully curled dasheen/callaloo bush or 1 bunch young tender spinach leaves

vegetable oil for frying

◆ Clean the dasheen/callaloo bush or spinach by removing the tips of the leaves, stems and veins. Wash thoroughly, and chop finely. Blanch in boiling water for about 2–3 minutes.

◆ Combine the phoulorie mixture with the dasheen/callaloo or spinach.

◆ Heat oil in a deep fryer, and drop the saheena mixture by heaped teaspoonfuls into the hot oil. Gently flatten with the back of a spoon. Fry until golden brown or until the saheena float to the top of the oil.

◆ Drain, and serve immediately with tamarind or mango chutney (see page 194).

Makes about 6 dozen

Cheesy party sandwiches

This cheese spread is a favorite at kids' birthday parties!

1 lb cheese, grated finely

3/4 lb butter

1 tsp yellow mustard

1 tsp pepper sauce

1 tbs chopped green olives

◆ Cream all the ingredients except the olives until a spreadable consistency is reached. Stir in the olives.

Party ribbon

◆ Trim crusts from 1 loaf unsliced white bread and 1 loaf unsliced brown bread. Cut each loaf horizontally into 6 slices.

◆ For each ribbon loaf, spread each of 2 slices of white bread and 1 slice brown bread with about ½ cup of the spread of your choice. Assemble the loaf, alternating white and brown slices. Top with a plain brown slice.

Appetizers

◆ Cut loaves into slices about ½ inch thick, then cut each slice crosswise into halves.

Makes about 10 dozen

Checkerboard

◆ Cut assembled ribbon loaves (above) into ½ inch slices.

◆ Spread butter or margarine on one slice, top with a second slice, placing the dark strip on top of the light. Press together gently.

Spread butter on top of the second slice, and top with a third slice with the light strip on top of the dark.

◆ Press and cut into 4 slices. Cut each slice into 2 sandwiches.

Makes 5 ½ dozen

Chili cheese puffs

½ cup unsalted butter, cut into cubes	1 cup grated sharp Cheddar cheese	½ tsp salt
1 cup water	1 tsp Dijon mustard	½ cup finely chopped chives
1 cup all-purpose flour	½ tsp yellow mustard	½ tsp minced garlic
4 eggs	1 tbs coarsely ground black pepper	¼ cup grated Parmesan cheese
	1 tsp chili powder	

◆ Preheat oven to 425°F.

◆ Place butter in water in a saucepan on low heat until butter melts. Bring to the boil. Remove pan from heat and add flour all at once. Stir quickly until dough comes together and forms a lump in the pan. There should be a skin at the base of your pan.

◆ Cook for about 5 minutes longer, then remove from heat and cool for about 5 minutes.

◆ Beat in eggs one at a time. Beat in Cheddar cheese and all the remaining ingredients, except for the Parmesan.

◆ Grease or line a baking sheet and drop teaspoonfuls of batter onto it. Sprinkle with Parmesan.

◆ Bake for about 25 minutes until puffed.

◆ Remove from oven and pierce puffs with a knife to release some steam. Return to oven for 5–10 minutes until dried out.

Makes about 15–18

Appetizers

Curry-flavored sardines with cilantro yogurt dip

1 lb fresh sardines, cleaned and washed in lime juice

2 cloves garlic, minced

1 cup flour

2 tsp curry powder

vegetable oil for frying

For the dip

½ cup natural yogurt

¼ cup low-fat mayonnaise

2 cloves garlic, minced

pepper sauce to taste

salt

1 tbs chopped chadon beni (cilantro)

◆ Combine sardines with the garlic, and season to taste with salt and freshly ground black pepper.

◆ Combine the flour and curry powder and season with salt and pepper.

◆ Heat oil in a frying pan or wok.

◆ Dredge sardines in flour mixture, drop into hot oil and fry until golden. Remove and drain.

◆ To prepare the dip, combine all the ingredients except for the chadon beni. Sprinkle with chadon beni and serve with the curry fried sardines.

Serves 4–6

Appetizers

Crab and avocado puffs

The season for avocados in the Caribbean runs from June through to September. The fruit are quite large and most varieties are buttery and wonderful.

For the puffs

½ cup unsalted butter, cut into cubes

1 cup water

1 cup all-purpose flour

4 eggs

1 tsp salt

For the filling

8 oz crabmeat

2 tbs lime juice

½ avocado, mashed

1 tbs sour cream

1 tbs mayonnaise

1 tsp hot pepper sauce

2 tbs finely chopped chives

¼ cup chopped chadon beni (cilantro)

◆ Preheat oven to 425°F.

◆ Place butter in water in a saucepan on low heat until butter melts, then bring to the boil.

◆ Remove pan from heat and add flour all at once. Stir quickly until dough comes together and forms a ball in the pan. Cook for about 5 minutes longer. There should be a film on the inside surface of the pan.

◆ Remove from heat. Beat in eggs one at a time, beating well between additions. Stir in the salt.

◆ Grease or line a baking sheet and drop teaspoonfuls of batter onto it, 1 inch apart.

◆ Bake for 20 minutes until puffed and dried. Cool and cut open.

◆ To prepare the filling, combine all the ingredients, except the chadon beni, and chill.

◆ Add the chadon beni just before serving. Fill the puffs and serve.

Makes 15–18

For a spicy variation on this recipe, add 1 teaspoon each chili powder and freshly ground black pepper to the puff ingredients. Spice up the filling by adding a teaspoon of chili powder. Omit the avocado and increase the quantity of mayonnaise to ½ cup.

Appetizers

Hummos with sesame

The Syrian/Lebanese influence in the Caribbean has made some familiar and delicious treats readily available!

1 can (14 oz) chickpeas (channa), drained and rinsed

2 tbs water (see method)

4 cloves garlic, minced

juice of 1 large lime

1 tbs natural yogurt

1/2 tsp pepper sauce or any hot pepper, seeded and chopped

1 tbs sesame oil

1 tsp ground roasted cumin (geera)

2 tbs chopped chadon beni (cilantro) or parsley

1 tbs olive oil

1 tsp sumac (optional)

black olives for garnishing

◆ Purée chickpeas coarsely in a food processor or blender. If you are using a blender, purée in 2 batches and add the water.

◆ Add the garlic, lime juice, yogurt, pepper sauce or hot pepper, sesame oil and cumin. Continue to purée mixture until smooth. Taste and add salt and freshly ground black pepper.

◆ Transfer to serving plate and sprinkle with chadon beni or parsley. Drizzle with olive oil then sprinkle with sumac, if using. Garnish with olives.

◆ Serve with warm pita bread or pita chips.

Serves 6

Pita chips

1 tsp salt

1 tsp freshly ground black pepper

1 tbs dried oregano

6 8 inch pitas

1/2 cup vegetable oil or olive oil

◆ Preheat oven to 400°F.

◆ Combine salt, pepper and oregano.

◆ Split open pita breads and cut each half into 8 wedges. Arrange on a baking sheet. Brush wedges lightly with oil, and sprinkle with dried herb mixture.

◆ Bake for 8–10 minutes until crisp.

Makes about 96

Appetizers

Cassava fritters

1 lb uncooked cassava, peeled, deveined and cut into small pieces

1 onion, chopped

4 cloves garlic

1/2 cup chopped chives, green and white parts

1/2 hot pepper, seeded and chopped, or 1 tsp pepper sauce, or to taste

1 tbs cornstarch

2 tsp baking powder

vegetable oil for frying

◆ Combine all the ingredients in a food processor and process to a fine paste. Season with salt and freshly ground black pepper to taste.

◆ Drop by teaspoonfuls into hot oil and fry until puffed and golden. Serve with chili pineapple dip.

Makes about 15

Peeling cassava/yuca. Run the edge of the knife lengthways down the cassava, making a small slit as you do so, then peel away both the brown rough skin and the pinkish skin. Your cassava should be white in color with no traces of skin. Cut the cassava into 2 inch lengths, then cut open and remove hard inner fiber.

Chili pineapple dip

1 cup low-fat mayonnaise

2 tbs fresh lime juice

1/2 cup chopped fresh pineapple

1 tsp chili powder

2 cloves garlic, minced

salt

1/4 cup chopped chadon beni (cilantro)

◆ Combine all of the above ingredients except the chadon beni. Sprinkle with chadon beni and serve with fritters.

Root vegetable chips

For this recipe you can use any type of root vegetable: cassava, dasheen, tannia, yams or sweet potato.

◆ Simply peel the vegetables and slice into papery thin slices. Fry each vegetable separately in hot oil and drain. Sprinkle with salt and serve as a snack.

Coconut fried shrimp *with fire and spice orange dip*

Adding the coconut milk powder to the batter brings out the coconut flavor in the shrimp.

> 3 lb large shrimp, cleaned with tails intact
>
> 2 cloves garlic, minced
>
> ½ tsp salt
>
> 2 cups all-purpose flour
>
> 1½ tsp baking powder
>
> 1 tbs coconut milk powder
>
> 1 tsp curry powder
>
> 1½ cups milk
>
> 2 cups finely shredded fresh coconut
>
> vegetable oil for frying

◆ Marinate shrimp in the garlic and salt.

◆ Make a smooth thick batter by combining 1½ cups flour, the baking powder, coconut milk powder and curry powder with the milk.

◆ Put the remaining ½ cup flour and the shredded coconut on 2 separate plates.

◆ Dredge each shrimp in flour, then dip into the batter, and then roll in the shredded coconut.

◆ Fry the shrimp in hot oil until golden. Drain and serve with orange dip.

Makes about 16

Fire and spice orange dip

> 1 cup orange marmalade
>
> ¼ tsp allspice
>
> ¼ tsp grated nutmeg
>
> juice of 1 orange
>
> ½ Congo pepper, seeded and minced (optional)
>
> 2 tsp Chinese chili sauce
>
> 1 tbs shredded ginger

◆ Combine all the ingredients. Serve with coconut fried shrimp.

Appetizers

Spinach and cheese turnovers

For the dough

4½ cups all-purpose flour

1 packet instant yeast (1 tbs)

1 cup milk

⅓ cup butter or margarine, melted

⅓ cup sugar

1 tsp salt

2 eggs

For the filling

2 tbs olive oil

1 large onion, finely chopped

3 cloves garlic, chopped

½ Congo (hot) pepper, seeded and chopped

1 lb fresh spinach, leaves only, washed and chopped

8 oz feta cheese or regular sharp Cheddar cheese or 4 oz Parmesan cheese

1 egg, lightly beaten

½ tsp grated nutmeg

salt and freshly ground black pepper

½ cup breadcrumbs

◆ Make the dough. In a mixer bowl combine 2 cups flour and the yeast.

◆ Heat the milk, butter, sugar and salt together to 115°–120°F. Add to flour mixture. Add eggs and beat slowly until incorporated. Add enough of the remaining flour to make a moderately stiff dough, then turn onto a floured surface and knead until it is smooth and elastic, about 6–8 minutes.

◆ Place in a greased bowl, cover and leave to rise until doubled in bulk, about 45 minutes.

◆ For the filling, heat the oil in a large skillet, add onion, garlic and pepper, and cook until fragrant and tender, about 10 minutes. Add spinach and cook until wilted.

◆ Transfer mixure to a bowl and cool slightly. Stir in crumbled cheese and egg, seasonings and breadcrumbs.

◆ Punch down the dough and leave to rest for 10 minutes.

◆ Preheat oven to 375°F.

◆ Divide dough into 24 equal pieces. Roll each piece into a 4 inch circle and place about 1 tablespoon of filling in the center of the lower half. Fold over and seal, pinching the edges together, using a little water if necessary. Place on a greased baking sheet. Repeat until all dough and filling are used up.

◆ Bake in preheated oven for 15–20 minutes until lightly browned.

Makes 24

Appetizers

Spice-marinated grilled shrimp
with spicy tomato salsa and plantain chips

2 lb large shrimp, peeled and deveined

For the marinade

1 tsp allspice

½ tsp grated nutmeg

1 tsp cinnamon

1 tsp ancho chili powder (or any good quality chili powder)

4 cloves garlic, minced

1 tbs fresh lime juice

2 tbs dark rum

◆ Prepare the marinade. In a bowl combine all the dried spices, then add garlic, lime juice and rum. Stir well to combine. Add salt and freshly ground black pepper to taste.

◆ Rub marinade onto shrimp, cover and refrigerate. Let marinate for about 30 minutes at most.

◆ Preheat broiler and thread shrimp onto metal skewers, or place shrimp in a shallow glass baking dish lightly oiled with olive oil. Broil for 3 minutes per side or until pink and slightly curled. Remove and serve with spicy tomato salsa (see page 192).

Serves 4

Plantain chips

4 green plantains

vegetable oil for frying

salt

◆ Peel plantains by cutting off tops and bottoms. With a small knife make a shallow incision into the plantain and run the knife the length of the plantain. Do this about three times around the plantain. Run your fingers down the length of the plantain where the cut has been made, lifting and pulling the skin off. The skin should lift off in pieces.

◆ Cut plantains in half and slice lengthways in about ¼ inch thick slices.

◆ Deep fry in hot oil on a medium heat until plantains are light brown and crisp.

◆ Drain on paper towels. Cool and sprinkle with salt. Store in an airtight container.

Serves 4–6

Appetizers

Spice-marinated grilled shrimp with Spicy tomato salsa (page 192) and Plantain chips

Crabmeat canapes

You could use baby salad shrimp in this recipe instead of the crab.
Steam them before using.

1 loaf sliced bread	*For the filling*	1 tsp pepper sauce
1 tbs butter or margarine	4 oz fresh or canned crabmeat, picked over	1 pimento pepper, seeded and chopped
sliced olives, red pepper strips, fresh herbs for garnishing	4 oz cream cheese	1 tbs chopped celery
	$\frac{1}{3}$ cup mayonnaise	1 tbs chopped chives
	1 tbs fresh lime or lemon juice	salt and freshly ground black pepper

◆ Cream all the filling ingredients together.

◆ Cut bread into shapes: squares, circles, triangles.

◆ Heat the butter or margarine in a frying pan, and lightly toast one side of the bread shapes in the frying pan.

◆ Spread untoasted side with filling. Garnish with olives, pepper strips and fresh herbs and serve.

Makes 15–20

Pastelles

These are stuffed cornmeal turnovers, wrapped in green fig leaves
and steamed to cook. A true delight to enjoy, they are traditionally served
at Christmas time in Trinidad and Tobago.

For the filling	2 tbs olive oil	1 tbs chopped celery
$\frac{1}{2}$ lb each ground (or chopped) beef and chicken	2 onions, finely chopped	$\frac{1}{4}$ cup tomato sauce
$1\frac{1}{4}$ tsp salt	4 cloves garlic, chopped	$\frac{1}{4}$ cup raisins
1 tsp freshly ground black pepper	2 pimento peppers, seeded and chopped	4 tbs capers
1 cup chopped chives	$\frac{1}{2}$ Congo pepper, seeded and chopped (optional)	3 tbs stuffed olives, sliced
3 tbs chopped thyme		

Appetizers

For the dough

2 cups yellow cornmeal

$^1/_2$ cup butter

$1^1/_4$ tsp salt

3 cups warm water

12 pieces of prepared fig leaves – 9 inch by 9 inch

string to tie pastelles

◆ Make the filling. Combine the beef with the chicken. Add salt, black pepper, $^1/_4$ cup chopped chives and 1 tablespoon thyme.

◆ Heat the olive oil in a large sauté pan. Add onion and garlic and sauté until fragrant. Add pimento peppers, Congo pepper, if using, the celery and the remaining chives and thyme. Add meat and cook until brown. Add tomato sauce, cover, and simmer for about 15 minutes.

◆ Add raisins, capers and olives and stir to combine. Cook for about 5 minutes more, taste and adjust seasoning. Remove from heat and leave to cool.

◆ In a food processor, or by hand, combine the cornmeal with the butter and salt, add water and process to make a soft, pliable dough.

◆ Divide the dough into 12 balls. Cover with a damp cloth to prevent drying.

◆ Place one piece of dough on a greased fig leaf, and press to an 8 inch width. Spoon 2 tablespoons filling onto the middle of the dough and fold and seal dough edges. Repeat until all the pastelles are made.

◆ Wrap fig leaf around and tie into a neat package. Steam pastelles for 45 minutes until cooked.

Makes 12

To prepare fig leaves, steam them in a large pot of boiling water for 10 minutes until they become pliable and soft.

Appetizers

Grilled chicken strips *with peanut sauce*

2 lb boneless chicken, cut into ½ inch by 3 inch strips

1 tsp saffron powder or turmeric

1 tbs sugar

1 tsp salt

1 tsp ground coriander

1 tsp ground cumin (geera)

1 tbs vegetable oil

2 cloves garlic

16 bamboo/wooden skewers, soaked in water

◆ Thread the chicken onto the skewers and place in a shallow bowl.

◆ Combine the rest of the ingredients in a food processor and blend until smooth. Pour over the chicken and marinate for 1 hour or more, turning frequently.

◆ Grill or barbecue for about 3 minutes on each side. Serve with peanut sauce.

Serves 4

Peanut sauce

2 tbs roasted peanuts

1 tsp lime juice

2 cloves garlic

4 tbs unsweetened coconut milk

4 tbs peanut butter

1 tsp sugar

1 tsp Chinese chili sauce

1 tbs soy sauce

1 tsp sesame oil

½ tsp ground coriander

½ tsp ground cumin (geera)

⅛ tsp turmeric

¼ cup chopped coriander or chadon beni (cilantro)

◆ Crush the peanuts in a food processor and set aside.

◆ Combine all the remaining ingredients except the coriander in processor and process until thoroughly blended.

◆ Transfer to a small bowl and sprinkle with the fresh coriander and ground peanuts. Cover and refrigerate until ready for use.

Appetizers

Spicy Caribbean nachos

8 cups large-cut corn chips

1 cup homemade or store-bought tomato salsa

½ cup chopped chives

1 onion, chopped

6 green olives, thinly sliced

½ hot pepper, seeded and chopped

1 green pepper, seeded and chopped

1 cup grated Cheddar cheese

¼ cup chopped chadon beni (cilantro)

½ cup thick yogurt or sour cream for serving

◆ Preheat oven to 400°F.

◆ Spread corn chips in a single layer on a large heatproof platter. Evenly distribute the salsa, chives, onion, olives, hot pepper and green pepper among the chips.

◆ Sprinkle the cheese over the top and place in preheated oven for about 10 minutes, just until the cheese melts and the chips have become crisp. Sprinkle on the chadon beni.

◆ Remove and serve at once with yogurt or sour cream.

Serves 4–6

Guacamole

Guacamole or avocado purée originated in Mexico, but it can be found in all areas of Central America, North America and the West Indies where avocados are grown. There is no basic recipe for guacamole as everyone has their favorite version of it. It is, however, considered in the ranks of salads to be the 'poor man's caviar'. It can be served as a dip with freshly cut veggies or corn chips, or as a garnish for Mexican dishes.

2 ripe avocados

4 cloves garlic, minced

1 tbs lime juice, or to taste

¼ cup sour cream or thick yogurt

salt and freshly ground black pepper

½ fresh hot pepper, seeded and finely chopped

¼ cup chopped chadon beni (cilantro) or coriander

2 tbs chopped chives

◆ Peel the avocados, and chop finely.

◆ In a mixing bowl combine the garlic, lime juice, sour cream, salt, black pepper, hot pepper and fresh coriander or chadon beni.

◆ Stir in the avocado and mix gently.

◆ Sprinkle with chives and serve.

Serves 8

Appetizers

Shrimp-filled avocados

1/4 cup good quality ketchup

1 tsp Worcestershire sauce

1 tbs chopped parsley

1 tbs chopped chives

1 tbs fresh lime or lemon juice

1 tsp Dijon mustard

2 cloves garlic, minced

1/2 cup low-fat mayonnaise

salt and freshly ground black pepper

1/2 tsp ground coriander

1/2 tsp pepper sauce, or to taste

1 lb cooked salad shrimp or small shrimp

4 small avocados

1/2 small lime

chopped chadon beni (cilantro) or coriander for garnishing

◆ In a small mixing bowl combine ketchup, Worcestershire sauce, herbs, lime or lemon juice, mustard, garlic, mayonnaise, salt, pepper, ground coriander and pepper sauce. Add shrimp and let marinate for about 30 minutes.

◆ Just before serving, cut avocados in half, remove stones and rub the cut portion with the lime half (a lemon works well here too). This will prevent them from changing color.

◆ Taste filling and adjust seasonings. Spoon into avocado halves and sprinkle with chopped chadon beni or coriander.

Serves 6–8

Chinese-style vegetable dumplings

1 tsp sesame oil

2 tbs soy sauce

1 tbs Chinese chili sauce

6 black dried Chinese mushrooms, soaked in warm water for 20 minutes

1/2 cup water chestnuts

2 tbs vegetable oil

2 tbs minced ginger

4 cloves garlic, chopped

1 cup grated carrot

1/2 cup chopped chives

1/2 cup bamboo shoots, chopped

1 pack wonton skins

Appetizers

◆ In a small bowl combine the sesame oil, soy sauce and chili sauce.

◆ Cut stems off mushrooms and chop. Chop the water chestnuts.

◆ Heat the vegetable oil in a wok or sauté pan, add ginger and garlic and sauté until fragrant. Add carrot and sauté for 1 minute. Add water chestnuts, chives, mushrooms and bamboo shoots. Sauté for 1 minute.

◆ Add sauce ingredients and stir to combine. Taste and adjust seasonings. Leave mixture to cool.

◆ Place a wonton skin on your counter top, spoon about 1 teaspoon of filling on bottom part of skin, fold over into a triangle shape and seal the edges with water. Repeat until all the filling has been used up.

◆ Steam for 15 minutes. Serve hot.

Makes about 25

Shrimp toasts with water chestnuts and mushrooms

6 water chestnuts

2 tbs parsley

1 tsp minced garlic

1 tbs chopped ginger

2 black dried Chinese mushrooms, soaked in hot water for 30 minutes

1 tsp sesame oil

2 tsp Chinese chili sauce

2 egg whites

1 tbs cornstarch

1 lb shrimp, peeled and deveined

1 tsp salt

6 slices white bread

vegetable oil for frying

◆ In a food processor process all the ingredients except the bread to a paste-like consistency.

◆ Trim crusts from bread. Spread bread with filling to about ½ inch thickness and cut into squares or triangles.

◆ Heat oil in a large frying pan, fry toasts until golden on both sides, drain, and serve with soy sauce or plum sauce.

Makes 24

Spicy shrimp with avocado cream

This is an elegant hors d'oeuvre – and the spice-rubbed shrimp makes it an exciting and vibrant one as well! The shrimp is served on pounded and fried plantains (see tostones, page 98).

½ tsp ground allspice

½ tsp grated nutmeg

½ tsp cinnamon

½ tsp chili powder

2 cloves garlic, minced

½ tbs fresh lime juice

¼ cup dark rum

½ lb shrimp, peeled and deveined

pounded and fried plantains for serving (see page 98)

chopped chadon beni (cilantro) for garnishing

For the avocado cream

½ avocado, mashed

½ tbs lime juice

1 clove garlic, minced

½ tsp Dijon mustard

¼ tsp ground cumin (geera)

salt and freshly ground black pepper

¼ small onion, minced

◆ In a bowl combine all the dried spices and add the garlic, lime juice and rum. Stir well to combine. Add salt and freshly ground black pepper to taste.

◆ Rub marinade onto shrimp, cover and refrigerate. Let marinate for about 30 minutes at most.

◆ Preheat broiler and place shrimp in a shallow glass baking dish, lightly oiled with olive oil. Broil for 3 minutes per side or until pink and slightly curled.

◆ To make the avocado cream, purée all ingredients and refrigerate until ready for use.

◆ Assemble by spreading the plantains with avocado cream and topping with shrimp. Sprinkle with chadon beni before serving.

Makes 12

Appetizers

Spicy shrimp with avocado cream

Caribbean vegetable tart

Flavors of the Mediterranean are available in the Caribbean. Basil and thyme grow quite well in herb gardens, and our red bell peppers are sun ripened.

2 tbs olive oil

1 large onion, sliced

2 tsp fresh thyme

2 tbs Dijon mustard

2 tbs pesto, made from basil

3–4 medium ripe tomatoes

1 large roasted red pepper, seeded and cut into strips

4 oz feta cheese, crumbled

For the dough

2 cups all-purpose flour

1 tsp salt

8 oz shortening or 4 oz each butter and shortening

½ cup iced water

◆ Make the dough. Place the flour and salt in the bowl of a food processor. Cut the shortening into small pieces and drop onto the flour. Pulse in food processor until mixture resembles fine crumbs.

◆ Add the water and pulse a few times, add more water and pulse again. Continue until the mixture has curds and clumps and sticks together when pressed between your fingers.

◆ Remove and form into a ball. Wrap and chill for at least 2 hours.

◆ Heat the oil in a small frying pan and sauté the onions with thyme until transparent, about 5 minutes. Remove and cool.

◆ Preheat oven to 400°F.

◆ Divide the dough into 8 equal pieces. Roll each piece into a 6 inch circle. Paint with Dijon mustard, then with pesto.

◆ Leaving a narrow margin around the dough (about ½ inch), place a small heap of tomatoes and onions on top, then some red pepper. Sprinkle with feta and season with salt and freshly ground black pepper.

◆ Fold the dough onto the vegetables as if making a package, but do not let the dough edges meet in the middle.

◆ Bake for 12–15 minutes until golden. Cool before serving.

Makes 8

Appetizers

Callaloo crepes

These are great as an appetizer. Serve them topped with a light tomato sauce.

For the crepes	For the filling	2 cloves garlic, chopped
1 cup cake flour	1¼ cups milk	½ Congo or hot pepper, seeded and chopped
⅛ tsp grated nutmeg	⅓ cup flour	
pinch salt	3 eggs, lightly beaten	1 small bunch callaloo/dasheen bush, leaves only, finely chopped, or 1 small bunch spinach, leaves only
⅔ cup milk	¼ cup grated Parmesan cheese	
⅔ cup water	¼ tsp grated nutmeg	
3 eggs	2 tbs vegetable oil	½ cup coconut milk
3 tbs melted butter	1 onion, chopped	

◆ Make the crepes. Mix together the flour, nutmeg and salt. Combine the milk and water. Add to flour mixture and whisk until smooth.

◆ Add the eggs one at a time, then whisk in the melted butter. Leave to rest for 10–30 minutes.

◆ Preheat a 6 inch frying pan, grease lightly and pour about ¼ cup of batter into the pan. Swirl to cover bottom of pan, if there seems too much batter in pan, pour off excess. When crepe appears dry around the edges, flip, cook for a few seconds more and remove. Repeat until all the batter is used, making about 10 crepes. Keep warm while making the filling.

◆ To make the filling, warm the milk in a small saucepan and gradually add the flour. Whisk and continue cooking until thick. Remove from heat and stir in eggs and cheese. Stir well to combine. Season to taste with salt, freshly ground black pepper and nutmeg. Set aside.

◆ Heat the oil in a sauté pan. Add onion, garlic and pepper, and sauté until tender. Add callaloo bush and stir. Add coconut milk slowly while callaloo is cooking.

◆ Cook for about 15–20 minutes until tender.

◆ Add callaloo to sauce mixture. Spoon mixture into crepes and roll. Place on plates and spoon tomato sauce over top.

Serves 4–6

Tomato sauce

2 tbs olive oil
1 large onion, chopped
4 cloves garlic, chopped
1 carrot, finely chopped
1 can (28 oz) tomatoes
1 tsp sugar
fresh basil or 1 tsp dried Italian herbs

Appetizers

◆ Heat the olive oil in a heavy saucepan, add onion and garlic and sauté until fragrant. Add the carrots and cook for 5 minutes longer. Add tomatoes, breaking them up with a spoon. Season with salt and freshly ground black pepper and add sugar. Add basil and continue to stir.

◆ Cover and simmer the sauce for about 1 hour, stirring occasionally.

◆ Taste and adjust seasonings.

Seasoned potato pies

ALOO PIES

These potato pies are always delicious, but the vendors' versions tend to be a little greasy. This version is delicious hot or at room temperature. Serve with chutney or kutchela.

For the dough

2 cups all-purpose flour

2 tsp baking powder

½ tsp salt

1 tbs butter

For the filling

1 lb potatoes, peeled and cut into quarters

2 cloves garlic, minced

1 pimento pepper, seeded and chopped

½ Congo pepper or hot pepper, seeded and chopped (optional)

2 tsp ground roasted cumin (geera)

pepper sauce to taste

1 small onion, finely chopped

¼ cup finely chopped chives

salt and freshly ground black pepper

vegetable oil for frying

◆ Make the dough by combining the flour with the baking powder, salt and butter. Add water to make a soft but pliable and non-sticky dough. Knead into a ball and let rest.

◆ Meanwhile, boil potatoes with a little salt until tender. When cooked, drain and crush well with a potato masher.

◆ Add garlic, peppers, cumin, pepper sauce, onion, chives, salt and pepper. Taste and adjust seasoning.

◆ Divide dough into 8 pieces, and shape each piece into a ball. Rest for 5 minutes.

◆ Roll each ball of dough into a 5 inch circle. Place about 1–2 tablespoons of the filling on to the lower portion of the circle, and bring the upper portion over lower portion to cover in a half moon shape. Seal, and continue until all the dough and filling is used up.

◆ Heat oil in a frying pan and shallow fry pies until golden brown. Drain and serve with chutney.

Makes 8

Appetizers

South American cornmeal turnovers

AREPAS

The original arepas from South America are just corn pancakes – these are the Caribbean version, stuffed with a delectable meat filling and fried!

For the dough

1 cup cornmeal

¼ cup flour

1 tsp salt

1½ tsp baking powder

1 tbs butter, softened

For the filling

½ lb ground beef

1 clove garlic, minced

2 tbs fresh thyme

salt and freshly ground black pepper

1 tbs vegetable oil

1 small onion, minced

½ hot pepper, seeded and chopped

⅓ cup raisins

1 tbs capers

2 tbs chopped olives

◆ Combine the cornmeal, flour, salt and baking powder in a mixing bowl. Add butter and rub into flour until mixture is like fine crumbs. Add enough water to make a soft but pliable dough.

◆ Rest the dough, covered, for 30 minutes.

◆ Form the dough into 12 equal size balls. Oil the dough balls and cover with a damp cloth until ready for use.

◆ Season meat with garlic, thyme, salt and pepper. Heat the oil in a sauté pan, add onion and sauté until soft, then add the hot pepper. Add meat and brown, then add raisins, capers and olives.

◆ Cover and finish cooking, adding a little water to prevent sticking, about 10 minutes. Leave to cool and divide into 12 portions.

◆ Press each dough ball into a circle about 5 inches in diameter (you may use a tortilla press here, but remember to place the dough between two pieces of waxed paper to prevent sticking). Place one portion of filling onto the center of the bottom half, fold over top half to cover bottom. Seal. Repeat until all the arepas are made.

◆ Fry in hot oil until light golden in color, about 4 minutes per side.

◆ Drain and serve with spicy salsa.

Makes 12

Baked meat and corn pies

For the dough

1 tbs granulated sugar

1 cup warm water (110°F)

1 tbs active dry yeast

1½ cups all-purpose flour

1½ cups cornmeal

1 tsp salt

¼ cup vegetable oil

For the filling

2 tbs vegetable oil

1 large onion, chopped

1 lb ground chicken or beef

1 tsp salt

3 tbs chili powder

1 tsp ground cumin (geera)

2 cups drained corn kernels

4 cloves garlic, minced

1 hot pepper, seeded and chopped

1 bell pepper, seeded and chopped

½ cup chopped chives

1 cup canned tomatoes, drained and chopped

3 cups grated cheese

½ cup chopped chadon beni (cilantro)

store-bought tomato salsa for serving

◆ Make the dough. In a small bowl dissolve the sugar in the water, sprinkle on the yeast and stir to dissolve. Let stand until bubbly, about 15 minutes. Meanwhile, in a large mixing bowl combine the flour, cornmeal and salt. Add the oil and the bubbly yeast mixture, combine, and knead until dough is smooth, elastic and shiny, about 15 minutes.

◆ Place the dough in an oiled bowl and cover with plastic wrap. Leave to rise for 60 minutes until doubled in bulk.

◆ Preheat oven to 400°F.

◆ Heat the oil in a large frying pan. Add the onion, and cook until translucent. Add chicken or beef and brown. Add salt, chili powder and cumin, and stir to combine. Stir in corn and cook for 10 minutes. Turn off the heat.

◆ Add garlic, hot pepper, bell pepper, chives and tomatoes. Taste and adjust seasonings.

◆ Divide cornmeal dough into 8 pieces. Roll each piece into an 8 inch round and brush with vegetable oil. Sprinkle half the circle with grated cheese and place meat mixture on top of cheese, leaving ½ inch border. Fold dough over and seal with a fork.

◆ Place on a lined baking sheet and repeat with the remaining dough.

◆ Bake for 15 minutes. Remove from oven, brush with vegetable oil, sprinkle with any remaining cheese and the chadon beni. Serve hot, accompanied by tomato salsa.

Makes 8

Appetizers

Soup and salad flavors

Soups in the Caribbean are thick, hearty, nourishing one-dish meals. The African influence permeates through most Caribbean soups with the use of lots of ground provisions or root vegetables, the most popular ones being eddoe, cassava, sweet potato and dasheen, dried peas and beans.

The most celebrated soup of the Caribbean, and every country will claim it as its own, is callaloo. This consists of a heady combination of callaloo leaves, ochroes, hot peppers, fresh herbs, coconut milk and some type of salted meat or fresh blue crab. Depending which island you're on you may find tiny dumplings in your soup.

Another favorite is sancoche, a name derived from South American stews called 'sancochos'. As the name implies, this soup is so thick that it can pass for a stew, made with up to nine different provisions, split peas, peppers, herbs and spices. It has become a Saturday lunch favorite in Trinidad and Tobago. Both there and also in Barbados dumplings are added to make it still heartier.

Pea and bean soups are very popular, as in Cuban black bean soup and Jamaican lentil soup. I've added cornmeal-cumin dumplings to my recipe for lentil soup to make it even more substantial.

Pumpkin soup is a favorite in Jamaica but can be found on most islands. Caribbean calabaza pumpkin, which is a dense, orange pumpkin, is preferred as it is less watery and is packed with flavor. Roasting the pumpkin also brings out the rich flavor in this soup.

Seafood, being ever popular, showcases itself in fish broth, also known as fish tea in Jamaica and soupe de poissons épice (spicy fish soup) in Martinique. This hot and spicy broth is infused with hot peppers and herbs, and is served with provisions and green figs.

The hot climate of the Caribbean does not encourage many fresh lettuce-based salads. Although 'green salads', as they are often called, may contain lettuce, they almost always include some type of cabbage, grated carrots and cucumbers. Many people prefer mayonnaise-based dressings, and potato and macaroni salads are very popular as well. I've lightened up these recipes to include some interesting and delicious alternatives like Grilled pineapple and sweet potato salad, Salad à la Caribbean, which is a French bistro salad with a Caribbean twist, and a tossed Caribbean salad sweetened with the addition of paw paw pieces.

Souse, which is an unusual vinegary soupy salad made with sliced cucumbers, hot peppers and usually pigs' trotters, is very popular in this area. I've omitted the pigs' trotters and added green figs, to make a lip-puckering, mouthwatering green fig souse. These green figs also make an interesting green fig salad dressed with a light vinaigrette in place of the traditional mayonnaise dressing.

Callaloo soup

CARIBBEAN SPINACH SOUP WITH OCHRO AND CRAB

A trademark of the Caribbean, this is a truly delightful soup. It can be enjoyed over rice or root vegetables at your main course or as a soup on its own.

2 tbs vegetable oil

1 medium onion, chopped

4 cloves garlic, minced

2 tbs chopped celery

1/4 cup fresh thyme

1/2 cup chopped chives

8 ochroes, sliced

1/2 cup chopped West Indian pumpkin

1 bunch dasheen bush or callaloo bush, washed and coarsely chopped, or 1 bunch spinach, washed and chopped

1 cup coconut milk

4 cups chicken stock or water

2 whole blue crab, cleaned and washed in lime juice, or 1 lb crabmeat

1 Congo pepper or hot pepper, left whole

2 tbs butter

◆ Heat the vegetable oil in a large heavy pot and add the onion, garlic, celery and fresh herbs. Sauté until fragrant, about 2 minutes. Add ochroes, pumpkin and dasheen leaves, and sauté for a further minute or so. Add coconut milk and stock or water and cook for a few minutes longer, then add whole crab and hot pepper.

◆ Bring to the boil and reduce heat to a simmer. Cook covered for about 50 minutes. Remove hot pepper, taste and add salt and freshly ground black pepper.

◆ Whisk soup until smooth. Stir in crabmeat, if using, and the butter. Simmer for 5 minutes more.

Serves 6–8

To make fresh coconut milk, crack your coconut and open. Remove any liquid inside the coconut.

With a strong knife remove the coconut flesh from the hard covering, the flesh will come away if you slide a knife between the flesh and the covering. Grate the flesh, or place it in a blender or food processor (I prefer the blender). Add 1 cup of hot water. Blend the coconut with the water. Set a sieve over a large bowl. Line sieve with a fine kitchen towel. Pour the blended coconut mixture into the sieve and squeeze out all the coconut milk. Repeat if necessary.

One coconut will yield 1 cup of coconut milk.

Soups . . .

Trini hearty corn soup

This true Trinidadian soup has got so popular that it has almost become a national dish! It's served as street food during Carnival time and at many if not most public parties and functions.

2 tbs vegetable oil

2 onions, chopped

3 cloves garlic, minced

1 lb English potatoes, peeled and quartered

2 carrots, diced

1/3 cup chopped chives

1/4 cup chopped celery

1/3 cup fresh thyme, chopped

2 pimento peppers, seeded and chopped

3/4 cup yellow split peas, washed and picked over

8 cups beef or vegetable stock

1 Congo pepper or hot pepper, left whole

1/2 cup coconut milk (optional)

6 ears corn, cut into 2 inch pieces

1 quantity dumplings, see right

1/2 cup chopped chadon beni (cilantro)

◆ Heat the oil in a large soup pot or Dutch oven. Add the onions and garlic and sauté until fragrant. Add the potatoes, carrots, chives, celery, thyme and pimento peppers, and cook for about 5 minutes more.

◆ Add split peas and stock, season with salt and freshly ground black pepper and bring to the boil. Add Congo pepper and coconut milk, if using. Cover and simmer for about 1 hour until peas are soft.

◆ Purée soup to a thick and creamy consistency, and return to pot. Add corn and dumplings and continue to cook for a further 20 minutes until corn is cooked and the dumplings float to the surface.

◆ Add chadon beni, remove from heat, taste and adjust seasonings. If soup seems too thick you can add a little water.

Serves 6–8

Dumplings

2 cups flour

1 tsp butter

2 tsp baking powder

1/2 tsp salt

◆ Place all the ingredients in a mixing bowl and rub butter into flour until mixture is grainy. Slowly add enough water to knead to a stiff dough. Cover and let rest for about 30 minutes.

◆ Divide dumpling dough into 2 pieces. Roll each piece into a long rope-like shape about 12 inches in length. Cut into 2 inch lengths and drop into boiling soup.

Makes about 12

Caribbean gumbo

1 tbs vegetable oil

2 tbs flour

4 cloves garlic, chopped

2 onions, chopped

4 tbs chopped celery

1 hot pepper, seeded and chopped

1 tsp paprika

1 red bell pepper, seeded and chopped

1 green bell pepper, seeded and chopped

3 cups chicken stock

1 can (28 oz) whole tomatoes, in their juice, chopped

4 oz chicken, chopped

6 oz okra, sliced

$\frac{1}{2}$ cup uncooked rice

1 cup corn niblets

$\frac{1}{2}$ lb small shrimp, peeled and deveined

◆ Heat the oil in a large heavy saucepan, add the flour and cook until medium brown in color, stirring constantly. Add garlic, onion and celery, hot pepper and paprika. Cook for a few seconds, add bell peppers and stock. Cook to boiling, then add tomatoes, chicken, okra and rice. Return to the boil, cover and cook until rice is tender, about 20 minutes.

◆ Season with salt and freshly ground black pepper. Add the corn and shrimp and cook for a further 5 minutes.

Serves 6–8

Soups...

Caribbean gumbo

Fresh tomato soup *with meat-filled dumplings*

A wonderful soup if you've got fresh and juicy tomatoes.

2 tbs vegetable oil

1 onion, chopped

2 cloves garlic, chopped

1 tbs chopped celery

1 carrot, chopped

6 large tomatoes, peeled, seeded and chopped, or 8 canned tomatoes

3 cups vegetable or chicken stock

$\frac{1}{2}$ tsp sugar

2 tbs chopped basil

2 tbs chopped chives

◆ Heat the oil in a saucepan, and add the onion, garlic, celery and carrot. Sauté until fragrant and tender, then add the tomatoes and stock and season with salt and freshly ground black pepper. Sprinkle on the sugar, cover and simmer until thick and soupy, about 30 minutes. Stir in the basil at the end of cooking and sprinkle over the chopped chives.

Serves 6

Meat-filled dumplings

$\frac{1}{4}$ lb ground beef, chicken or veal

1 tbs minced chives

salt and freshly ground black pepper

1 clove garlic, minced

$\frac{1}{2}$ tbs vegetable oil

1 quantity dumpling dough (see page 31)

◆ Season the meat with chives, salt, pepper and garlic.

◆ Heat the oil in small sauté pan or skillet, add seasoned meat and sauté until meat loses its pinkness. Remove from heat and cool.

◆ Cut dumpling dough into 12 pieces. Make each piece into a round and shape into a $2\frac{1}{2}$–3 inch circle. Place about 1 teaspoon of meat into the lower half of the dough. Fold other half over and seal. Repeat until all the dumplings have been filled.

◆ Drop dumplings into boiling soup and cook for 10 minutes until puffed.

Soups . . .

Sancoche

Sancoche is a local Trinidadian soup that is so very hearty it is really more of a stew. It's made with lots of ground or root vegetables, often with pig's tail or beef bones, and split peas.

2 lb ground provision (sweet potatoes, yams, eddoes, cassava)

3 tbs vegetable oil

2 onions, chopped

3 tbs chopped celery

2 pimento peppers, seeded and chopped

¼ cup fresh thyme

1 lb stewing beef with bones, seasoned with 1 tbs minced chives and 2 minced cloves garlic

1 cup yellow split peas

6 ochroes, sliced

1 cup chopped pumpkin

8 cups beef stock

1 plantain, half-ripe, peeled and thickly sliced

1 Congo pepper or habanero pepper, left whole

dumplings (see page 31)

◆ Peel provision and cut into 2 inch pieces. Place in a bowl and cover with water until ready to use.

◆ Heat the oil in a large soup pot or Dutch oven, add onions, celery, pimento pepper and thyme. Sauté until fragrant. Add beef and stir until browned. Add split peas, ochroes and pumpkin, sauté, then add stock and simmer until split peas are cooked to a nice thickness and beef is tender, about 1 hour. Season with salt and freshly ground black pepper.

◆ Add provision, plantain and hot pepper, and cook until provision is tender, about 30 minutes.

◆ Drop in dumplings and cook until dumplings have floated to the top of the pot, about 10–15 minutes. Serve hot with or without the hot pepper.

Serves 6–8

Vegetarian sancoche

2 lb ground provision (sweet potatoes, yams, eddoes, cassava)

3 tbs vegetable oil

2 onions, chopped

2 cloves garlic, minced

2 tbs chopped celery

2 pimento peppers, seeded and chopped

¼ cup fresh thyme

1 cup yellow split peas

6 ochroes, sliced (optional)

1 cup chopped carrot

1 cup chopped pumpkin

8 cups vegetable stock

1 Congo pepper or hot pepper, left whole

dumplings (see page 31)

1 plantain, half-ripe, peeled and thickly sliced

◆ Peel provision and cut into 2 inch pieces. Place in a bowl and cover with water until ready to use.

◆ Heat the oil in a large soup pot or Dutch oven, add the onions, garlic, celery, pimento pepper and thyme. Sauté until fragrant, then add split peas, ochroes if using, carrot and pumpkin and stir. Add stock and simmer until split peas are cooked to a nice thickness, about 1 hour. Season with salt and freshly ground black pepper.

◆ Add provision and hot pepper and cook until tender, about 20 minutes.

◆ Drop in the dumplings and add plantain. Cook until dumplings and plantain are cooked, about 10 minutes. Serve hot with or without the hot pepper.

Serves 6–8

Cuban black bean soup

Cubans love to cook with black beans and this soup is just one of the many delicious ways in which they use them.

2 tbs vegetable oil

4 cloves garlic, chopped

1 large onion, chopped

1 cup black beans, soaked overnight and drained

1 tsp ground cumin (geera)

1 hot pepper, seeded (optional)

1 tsp chili powder

salt and freshly ground black pepper

8 cups vegetable stock

¼ cup chopped chadon beni (cilantro)

½ cup sour cream or natural yogurt

◆ Heat the oil in a large soup pot or saucepan. Add garlic and onion and sauté until fragrant. Add the drained black beans together with the cumin, hot pepper, if using, chili powder, salt and pepper.

◆ Add the stock, cover and cook until beans are tender, about 1 hour.

◆ Purée half the soup in a blender and combine with the other half.

◆ Taste and adjust seasonings. Serve in soup plates garnished with the chadon beni and a dollop of the sour cream or yogurt.

Serves 4–6

Lentil soup with cornmeal-cumin dumplings

1 tbs vegetable oil

4 cloves garlic, chopped

⅓ cup chopped celery

¼ cup fresh thyme

1 large onion, chopped

½ hot pepper, seeded and chopped

1 carrot, finely chopped

1 tsp ground cumin (geera)

1 lb brown lentil peas, washed and picked over

9 cups vegetable stock or water

◆ Heat the oil in a large stock pot or saucepan. Add the garlic, celery, thyme, onions and hot pepper. Sauté until fragrant. Add carrots, cumin and lentils and sauté for a few more minutes.

◆ Add the stock, cover and then simmer until lentils are soft and melted, about 40–50 minutes.

Serves 6–8

Cornmeal-cumin dumplings

1 cup flour

1 cup cornmeal

1 tsp baking powder

1½ tsp ground roasted cumin (geera)

½ tsp salt

2 tbs butter

◆ Combine all the ingredients in a bowl and cut butter into flour until texture is grainy. Add enough water to make a pliable dough. Gently press the dough into a circle about ¾ inch thick. Cut into small 1 inch squares and drop into the boiling soup. Cook until puffed and light, about 10 minutes.

Caribbean fish broth

1 lb fresh fish fillets, cut into 1 inch chunks

2 tsp minced chives

salt and freshly ground black pepper

2 tbs vegetable oil

1 small onion, chopped

2 pimento peppers, seeded and chopped

2 tbs chopped thyme

3 cups ground provision (dasheen, cassava, eddoes), cut into chunks

4 green figs, peeled and cut into 2 inch pieces

1/3 cup chopped chadon beni (cilantro)

1 Congo pepper

For the broth

7 cups water

1 large fish head and center bone

1 Congo pepper or hot pepper, left whole

2 pimento peppers, left whole

1/4 cup fresh thyme

1 onion, chopped

2 cloves garlic

salt and freshly ground black pepper

◆ Marinate fish pieces in minced chives, salt and pepper.

◆ Make the broth. Put the water in a large soup pot and add all the other ingredients. Bring to the boil and simmer for 1 hour. Strain and reserve.

◆ Heat the oil in a large soup pot, and add the onion, pimento peppers and thyme. Add provisions and green figs and turn, then add the strained fish broth, chadon beni and Congo pepper.

◆ Bring to the boil, cover and simmer for 15–20 minutes until provisions are cooked.

◆ Gently drop in fish chunks and cook for a further 5 minutes until fish is cooked. Remove whole Congo pepper before serving.

Serves 6–8

Soups . . .

Roasted pumpkin soup

1½ lb pumpkin, preferably calabaza	4 cloves garlic	1 tsp salt, or to taste
2 tbs vegetable oil	½ hot pepper, seeded and chopped	2 cups milk
1 small onion, finely chopped	2 tbs flour	sour cream or natural yogurt for serving
¼ cup chopped chives	2 cups chicken stock or water	

◆ Preheat oven to 400°F.

◆ Slightly oil the pumpkin and place on a baking sheet. Bake for 40–60 minutes until tender. Peel and remove flesh, then purée in a food processor.

◆ Heat the oil in a saucepan, add onion, chives, garlic and pepper and cook until fragrant. Add flour and stir to make a smooth roux.

◆ Add stock and bring to the boil. Season with salt and freshly ground black pepper, then add puréed pumpkin and cook until mixture is thick.

◆ Purée mixture in a blender to a smooth consistency. Return to pot and add milk. Stir to heat through.

◆ Serve with a dollop of sour cream or yogurt, and garnish with chopped chives.

Serves 4–6

Cream of cucumber soup

4 tbs butter

1 onion, chopped

3 cucumbers, peeled and sliced

3 tbs flour

3 cups vegetable or chicken stock

1 cup milk

chopped mint or chives for garnishing

◆ Melt 2 tablespoons of the butter in a medium-sized saucepan and sauté the onion and cucumbers until cucumbers become tender and the onion is fragrant. Remove from pot.

◆ Melt the remaining butter and add flour. Cook to a smooth roux, add stock and stir, cooking over low heat until thick. Season with salt and freshly ground black pepper.

◆ Return cucumbers and onion to pot and cook for a further 10 minutes.

◆ Purée soup in a blender. Just before serving, heat and stir in the milk. Garnish with chopped mint or chives.

Serves 4–6

Breadfruit vichyssoise

2 tbs butter

2 cloves garlic, chopped

2 pimento peppers, seeded and chopped

$1/2$ hot pepper, seeded and chopped

$1/2$ cup chopped chives

1 large onion, chopped

2 cups uncooked breadfruit, cut into cubes

4 cups chicken stock

$1/4$ tsp grated nutmeg

$1/4$ tsp white pepper

1 cup milk

◆ Melt butter in a heavy saucepan, add garlic, peppers, chives and onions. Cook until tender.

◆ Add the breadfruit and stir to combine. Add stock and season with nutmeg, salt and white pepper. Bring to the boil, cover and simmer until breadfruit is tender, about 20 minutes.

◆ Purée soup in a blender or food processor. Add the milk and stir. If still a little thick you can add a little more stock.

◆ The soup may be served at room temperature or hot.

Serves 4–6

Soups . . .

Salad à la Caribbean

8 cups mixed salad greens, cleaned, washed, dried and broken into bite-sized pieces

¼ cup olive oil

6 slices French bread, cubed

6 oz Cheddar cheese, cubed

2 tbs chopped mixed herbs (parsley, basil, chives or cilantro)

1 large ripe tomato, cut into segments

1 cucumber, sliced

For the dressing

3 tbs red wine vinegar

2 cloves garlic, minced

1 tbs Dijon mustard

salt and freshly ground black pepper

½ cup extra virgin olive oil

◆ Place greens in a large salad bowl.

◆ Heat the olive oil in a skillet and brown the bread cubes. Season with salt and freshly ground black pepper. Remove and drain.

◆ Sprinkle the salad greens with the cheese, bread, and herbs. Add tomato and cucumber.

◆ Make the dressing. In a small bowl whisk together the vinegar, garlic, mustard, salt and black pepper. Add olive oil and continue whisking until well combined.

◆ Toss salad with the dressing. Serve immediately.

Serves 6

Grilled pineapple and sweet potato salad

1 lb sweet potatoes

½ medium pineapple, peeled, cored and cut into 1 inch chunks

1 cup mixed fresh herbs (basil, chives, chadon beni or parsley)

1 large red or green bell pepper, seeded and cut into strips

For the vinaigrette

juice of 1 lemon

¼ cup sunflower oil

1 tsp Dijon mustard

1 clove garlic, minced

salt and freshly ground black pepper

◆ Preheat broiler.

◆ Combine all ingredients for the vinaigrette and set aside.

◆ Boil or roast sweet potatoes until tender. Drain and cool. Peel and cut into 1 inch cubes.

◆ Place pineapple in a glass dish and broil or grill for 10 minutes, turning frequently. Remove and cool.

◆ Combine herbs, peppers, pineapple and potatoes, toss with the vinaigrette and season to taste with salt and freshly ground black pepper. Chill.

Serves 4–6

To roast sweet potatoes, wash, wrap in foil and place in a preheated 350°F oven for about 45–50 minutes or until tender.

Soups . . .

Grilled pineapple and sweet potato salad

Tossed Caribbean salad with paw paw

8 cups mixed salad greens, cleaned, washed, dried and broken into bite-sized pieces

2 tbs chopped mixed herbs (parsley, basil, chives or chadon beni)

1 cup cubed paw paw, firm but ripe

1 small cucumber, peeled and sliced

2 tomatoes, cut into quarters

1/4 red onion, thinly sliced

For the dressing

3 tbs red wine vinegar

2 cloves garlic, minced

1 tsp Dijon mustard

salt and freshly ground black pepper

1/2 cup extra virgin olive oil

◆ Place all the salad ingredients in a large salad bowl.

◆ In a small bowl whisk together the vinegar, garlic, mustard, salt and pepper. Add olive oil and continue whisking until well combined.

◆ Toss salad with dressing and serve immediately.

Serves 6

Green fig souse

8 green figs

vegetable oil

4 tbs fresh lime juice

1 large onion, thinly sliced

2 cloves garlic, minced

1 hot pepper, seeded and thinly sliced

salt and freshly ground black pepper

2 cucumbers, peeled and thinly sliced

◆ Place green figs in a non-reactive heavy saucepan. Add a little oil and boil for about 15 minutes until tender. Remove and leave to cool. Then peel and slice.

◆ Place figs in a glass bowl, add all other ingredients except cucumber, and pour on boiling water just to cover figs. Cool and refrigerate overnight.

◆ Fifteen minutes before serving, add the cucumber slices.

Serves 6

Soups...

Green fig vinaigrette

12 green figs

4 cloves garlic, minced

½ Congo pepper, seeded and finely chopped

¼ cup apple cider vinegar or red wine vinegar

juice of 1 lime

½ tsp Dijon mustard

salt and freshly ground black pepper

¾ cup olive oil

1 onion, finely sliced

1 red pepper, seeded and chopped

1 green pepper, seeded and chopped

½ cup finely chopped mint or parsley

◆ Place green figs in a non-reactive heavy saucepan, add a little oil, and boil for about 15 minutes until tender. Remove and leave to cool. Then peel and slice.

◆ In a food processor combine the garlic, Congo pepper, vinegar, lime juice, mustard, salt and pepper. Purée until smooth.

◆ Add olive oil and process until all ingredients are incorporated and smooth.

◆ Toss green figs with vinaigrette, add onion and green and red peppers. Toss again, sprinkle on fresh herbs and serve.

Serves 4–6

Grilled vegetable and chicken pasta salad with basil

4 boned chicken thighs

1 tbs minced basil plus ½ cup chopped basil

8 cloves garlic, minced

¼ cup olive oil

2 tbs red wine vinegar

salt and freshly ground black pepper

1 medium eggplant

1 sweet red bell pepper

1 onion, peeled

1 cup fresh mushrooms

1 lb pasta, cooked and drained

◆ Marinate chicken in the minced basil and 2 minced cloves of garlic. Let stand for 30 minutes.

◆ Preheat broiler.

◆ Broil chicken for about 8–10 minutes each side. Cool, then cut into strips.

◆ Preheat grill to medium setting.

◆ Combine olive oil, remaining garlic, vinegar, salt and pepper, and whisk together.

◆ Slice the eggplant into ¼ inch thick slices. Then rub all the vegetables with about 2 tablespoons of the marinade and let sit for about 30 minutes.

◆ Grill until tender. Then chop vegetables into strips and combine with the remaining marinade, chicken and pasta. Sprinkle with chopped basil and serve.

Serves 4–6

Soups . . .

Meat flavors

Chicken is the most popular meat used in the Caribbean, where it is eaten in many ways, from barbecue to jerk, from curry to stew, roasted, stuffed, and stirfried, reflecting many different influences. Beef, goat and lamb are also favorites.

Cooking Caribbean meats usually begins with a marinating process for the meat. Wet herb marinades or herb pastes are a mainstay in many Caribbean kitchens. A herb marinade, or 'green seasoning' as it is often called, often includes a ground mixture made from fresh chives, thyme, garlic, parsley, celery and marjoram. Cooks in Barbados like to add grated nutmeg to the mixture. The wet paste is rubbed onto the meat before cooking. When cooking stews, an African method of caramelizing sugar in oil before adding the meat is used quite a bit. This gives the meat a rich, golden color. Many cooks prefer to use brown cane sugar as opposed to white granulated sugar.

Jerk marinade, indigenous to Jamaica, can now be found in most Caribbean countries. Originally, jerking the meat, or cooking in a smoke-dry method, was used in Jamaica as a way to preserve meat. Today it has become part of Jamaica's culinary heritage and commercial jerk marinade can be found in any grocery store anywhere!

Curries are popular on the islands and reflect the heavy East Indian heritage here. The most popular are the commercial curry powders made with turmeric, fenugreek, coriander, cumin, hot pepper, black peppercorns, anise, cloves and mustard seed. Curried goat is a great favorite in Grenada,

Jamaica and Trinidad and Tobago, where it is sometimes cooked with a little coconut milk and is often served as part of East Indian wedding feasts. I've added a little yogurt to the goat when marinating and this serves to produce an even more tender and succulent meat.

Roasted lamb is a favorite on the Dutch islands of Aruba and Curaçao. My favorite take on lamb is roasting a leg, or barbecuing chops. A delicious lamb stew is always welcomed in these areas as well. Cuban lamb and black bean chili makes a spicy alternative to the traditional Mexican chili con carne.

Beef is often served curried or stewed and is also included in Chinese stirfries.

Easy barbecued chicken and lamb

Many people like to pre-cook their chicken before placing it on the barbecue pit. I think a lot of the flavor of the barbecue is lost this way. For the best barbecue chicken, marinate your bird about 4 hours prior to cooking and cook on a medium setting on the barbecue pit, turning frequently to prevent charring. You will have to have a spritzer bottle filled with water to prevent flare-ups.

Chicken

1 whole chicken, 3 lb, cut into quarters

2 tbs minced garlic

2 tbs olive oil

1 tbs red wine vinegar

freshly ground black pepper

◆ Combine ingredients for marinade and rub into the chicken pieces. Allow to marinate for 4 hours or overnight. Grill as described above. The chicken will be cooked in about 20–30 minutes. Brush with barbecue sauce and serve.

Serves 3–4

Lamb

2½–3 lb lamb shoulder

½ cup teriyaki sauce

1 tbs minced garlic

freshly ground black pepper

◆ Slice the lamb shoulder cut 1 inch thick. Combine the marinade ingredients and pour over the lamb. Allow to marinate for 4 hours or overnight. Place the lamb on high heat and grill for 4 minutes per side, brushing with barbecue sauce.

Serves 3–4

Cornmeal and cumin crusted chicken
with mango lime salsa

1 lb boneless chicken breasts

2 tsp minced garlic

1 tsp salt

1 tsp freshly ground black pepper

1 cup cornmeal

1 tbs ground cumin (geera)

1 egg

½ cup flour

vegetable oil for frying

◆ Pound the chicken breasts to about ¼ inch thickness and cut into strips about 3 inches by 1½ inches. Rub the chicken with the garlic, half the salt and the pepper.

◆ Combine the cornmeal with the cumin and remaining salt.

◆ Beat the egg lightly.

◆ Dredge chicken in flour, dip into the egg, then coat with cornmeal mixture.

◆ Shallow fry in vegetable oil until golden. Drain and serve with mango lime salsa.

Serves 4–6

Mango lime salsa

2 cups finely chopped (half-ripe) mango, preferably Julie mango

1 tbs fresh lime juice

1 clove garlic, minced

¼ cup chopped chadon beni (cilantro)

2 tbs chopped chives

½ hot pepper, seeded and finely chopped, or to taste

salt

◆ Combine all the ingredients in a glass bowl and refrigerate until ready for use.

Makes about 2 cups

Caribbean ginger chicken

juice and zest of 1 lime

juice of 1 orange

2 tbs honey

2 tbs grated ginger

4 cloves garlic, minced

½ tsp cinnamon

1 tsp pepper sauce

2 lb chicken pieces

1 tbs vegetable oil

1 can (8 oz) tomatoes, crushed with juices

◆ Combine the lime juice, orange juice and honey. Add ginger, garlic, cinnamon and pepper sauce.

◆ Add marinade to chicken pieces and rub in well. Cover and refrigerate for 2 hours.

◆ Heat the oil in a large sauté pan. Add the chicken pieces, one at a time, reserving the marinade, and brown on each side. Pour on reserved marinade, add the tomatoes and lime zest and season with salt and freshly ground black pepper.

◆ Cover and simmer until cooked, about 20 minutes, turning pieces occasionally.

◆ Remove the chicken pieces, increase the heat on the pan and reduce juices to a nicely thickened sauce. Pour over chicken and serve.

Serves 4–6

Meat

Stuffed chicken breasts

*This stuffing recipe is great to stuff a whole bird if you prefer.
These are quite elegant though!*

4 cloves garlic

½ tsp freshly ground black pepper

1½ lb boneless chicken breasts (about 6 chicken breasts)

2 tbs vegetable oil

1 large onion, finely chopped

½ cup chopped chives

2 pimento peppers, seeded and chopped

2 tbs fresh thyme

2 cups fresh breadcrumbs

2 tbs raisins

about ½ cup chicken stock

¼ cup grated cheese (optional)

¼ cup chopped parsley

◆ Mince 2 cloves garlic and combine with black pepper.

◆ Prepare chicken breasts by placing each piece between two sheets of waxed paper. Pound the breasts until about ¼ inch thick. Season with the garlic and black pepper mixture.

◆ Prepare the stuffing. Heat half the oil in a large sauté pan, add remaining garlic, chopped, and the onion. Sauté until fragrant, then add chives, pimento peppers and thyme. Stir and fry for 4 minutes until all the herbs become fragrant.

◆ Add the breadcrumbs and raisins. Stir to combine, then gradually add a small amount of chicken stock at a time Stir until stuffing comes together. Add cheese, if using, and parsley. Stir and mix. Taste and adjust seasoning, then leave to cool.

◆ Preheat oven to 350°F.

◆ Place about 1 tablespoon of stuffing on each chicken breast, roll each breast up and hold together with small metal skewers.

◆ Heat remaining oil in sauté pan and sauté chicken breasts until brown. Remove to a heatproof baking dish and bake for 30 minutes.

◆ Remove chicken breasts from dish and remove skewers. Cool, then slice and serve. (You could make a sauce using the drippings from the baking dish.)

Serves 6

Island stirfry with pineapple and mushrooms

½ cup dried Chinese black mushrooms

1½ lb boneless chicken breasts

4 tbs vegetable oil

1½ tbs minced ginger

1 tbs minced garlic

2 tbs minced chives

1 cup pineapple chunks

For the marinade

2 tbs soy sauce

1 tbs white wine or rice wine

1 tbs minced garlic

1 tsp sesame oil

1 tsp cornstarch

For the sauce

½ cup chicken stock or mushroom water

½ tbs white wine or rice wine

1 tsp sugar

½ tbs soy sauce

1 tsp sesame oil

1½ tsp cornstarch

◆ Soak mushrooms in about 1 cup hot water for 20 minutes.

◆ Slice chicken into ¼ inch thick slices.

◆ Combine marinade ingredients in a small bowl. Place chicken in marinade and stir to combine. Let sit for at least 30 minutes.

◆ Drain mushrooms and reserve the liquid. Remove stems from mushrooms and slice.

◆ Combine the sauce ingredients and stir well.

◆ Heat 2 tablespoons of the oil in a wok or skillet. When hot, add chicken and stirfry until it loses its pink color. Remove from wok. Clean out pan.

◆ Heat the remaining oil in wok or skillet. Add the ginger, garlic and chives and stirfry until fragrant. Add black mushrooms and pineapple and stirfry for a few minutes. Return chicken to pan, add sauce and cook until sauce thickens.

◆ Remove from pan, taste and adjust salt to taste. Serve with rice.

Serves 4 6

Meat

Caribbean jerk chicken

4 lb chicken

3 tbs allspice berries, ground

2 hot peppers (habenero, Congo or Scotch bonnet)
or more to taste, seeded and chopped

8 blades chive, green and white parts

1 large onion, chopped

8 cloves garlic

2 inch piece of ginger

1/3 cup fresh thyme

1/2 tsp grated nutmeg

1 tsp cinnamon

1/2 tbs freshly ground black pepper

2 tbs lime juice

1/3 cup vegetable oil

◆ Wash the chicken and cut it into quarters.

◆ In a blender or food processor process the rest of the ingredients to a smooth paste.

◆ Rub about 2 tablespoons marinade over chicken pieces to completely cover all parts – use more marinade if necessary.

◆ Cover and refrigerate for 4 hours or overnight. Add salt if wished.

◆ Preheat oven to 350°F.

◆ Bake chicken, turning once, for about 20–30 minutes until the juices run clear. This chicken may be cooked over hot coals as well.

Serves 4–6

Meat

Caribbean jerk chicken with Jamaican rice and peas (page 114)

Meat

Carnival chicken

For a lighter dish just omit the cheese and serve with additional salsa.

2 whole chicken breasts, skinned, boned and cut into about 3 pieces each, depending on the size of the chicken

1 tsp minced garlic

1 tbs minced chives

salt and freshly ground black pepper

⅓ cup flour

1 tsp chili powder

½ tsp ground cumin (geera)

2 tbs vegetable oil

spicy tomato salsa (see page 192)

1 cup grated Cheddar cheese

2 tbs chopped chadon beni (cilantro)

◆ Preheat broiler.

◆ Place one piece of chicken between 2 sheets of waxed paper and with a rolling pin slightly pound chicken to ¼ inch thickness. Repeat with the other pieces.

◆ In a small mixing bowl combine the garlic, chives, salt and pepper. Rub mixture over chicken pieces.

◆ On a small plate combine the flour, chili powder and cumin. Coat the chicken pieces in the flour mixture.

◆ Heat the oil in a non-stick frying pan and cook chicken until browned on each side. Remove from heat and drain.

◆ Place chicken in a baking dish. Reduce heat and spoon 1 tablespoon of the salsa on top of each chicken piece. Sprinkle evenly with cheese and place under broiler for a few seconds until cheese melts.

◆ Serve with the chadon beni sprinkled over the top.

Serves 2–4

Meat

Stuffed chicken thighs

3/4 cup bulgur wheat

3/4 cup cold water

4 sun-dried tomatoes, soaked in warm water for about 30 minutes

3 tbs olive oil

1 tsp salt

4 cloves garlic, minced

8 chicken thighs or drumsticks

1/2 cup chopped onion

1 pimento pepper, seeded and chopped

1/3 cup chopped chives

1/2 cup chopped parsley

1/2 tsp freshly ground black pepper

2 tbs butter

◆ Soak bulgur wheat in the cold water for 1 hour. Drain, and squeeze out excess moisture.

◆ Drain tomatoes and chop.

◆ Mix 1 tablespoon olive oil with the salt and half the garlic. Rub into chicken and set aside.

◆ Sauté the onion with the rest of the garlic and the pimento in remaining oil until fragrant, about 5 minutes. Add the sun-dried tomatoes, remove from heat, add bulgur and combine. Add chives, parsley and black pepper. Add salt to taste. Remove from pan and cool.

◆ Make an incision into the meatiest part of each thigh and fill with about 1 1/2 tablespoons of stuffing.

◆ Preheat oven to 375°F.

◆ Heat butter in a sauté pan, place chicken pieces in pan and sauté until brown on all sides.

◆ Place chicken in a casserole dish and bake for 30 minutes until cooked.

Serves 4–6

Chicken and okra rice

2 tbs vegetable oil

1/2 chicken, seasoned with ground chive and garlic, cut into pieces

2 cups chopped onion

4 cloves garlic, chopped

1 hot pepper, seeded and chopped

2 pimento peppers, seeded and chopped

8 okra, sliced

2 cups rice

4 1/2 cups chicken or vegetable stock

1/2 cup coconut milk, or 2 tbs coconut milk powder

Meat

◆ Heat the oil in a large sauté pan. Add the chicken pieces and brown. Add onion, garlic and peppers and sauté until fragrant. Add okra and cook for about 5 minutes.

◆ Add the rice and turn to coat rice grains with oil and flavorings. Add stock and coconut milk and stir to combine. Bring to the boil and cover.

◆ Cook for about 20 minutes until rice grains are tender. Taste and adjust seasonings.

Serves 6–8

Citrus baked chicken

1 small pineapple, cut into chunks

1 hot pepper, seeded and chopped

2 cloves garlic

1 cup fresh orange juice

½ cup fresh lime juice

½ tsp cinnamon

2 tbs chopped parsley

1 tbs freshly ground black pepper

1 tsp grated orange peel

1 tsp grated lime peel

3½–4 lb chicken, cut into pieces

2 tbs honey

⅓ cup butter

◆ Purée the pineapple, hot pepper and garlic in a blender until smooth. Add orange juice, lime juice, cinnamon, parsley, black pepper, orange and lime peel. Stir to combine.

◆ Pour over chicken in a glass container and rub marinade into chicken pieces. Cover and refrigerate for 4 hours or overnight, turning the chicken pieces occasionally.

◆ Remove chicken from marinade and scrape off any excess. Strain marinade into a heavy saucepan, remove ⅓ cup and mix with the honey.

◆ Boil remaining marinade until reduced to about 1½ cups. Whisk in butter, and season with salt and pepper.

◆ Preheat grill and grill chicken until cooked for about 5 minutes per side, brushing with the reserved honey marinade.

◆ Serve with sauce separately.

Serves 8

Oven-roasted chicken with island spice rub

Wet marinades are more popular in the Caribbean, but with the availability of good quality dried spices, dried rubs are becoming popular as well!

1 tbs olive oil

1 tbs minced chives

3 cloves garlic, minced

3½ lb chicken, cut into quarters, or 4 lb chicken pieces

For the rub

⅓ cup ground roasted cumin (geera)

⅓ cup chili powder

4 tbs ground crushed coriander seeds

1 tbs cinnamon

1 tsp grated nutmeg

½ tbs brown sugar

2 tbs salt

2 tbs freshly ground black pepper

1 tsp cayenne pepper (optional)

1 tsp paprika

◆ In a spice mill or food processor or blender, process all the ingredients for the spice rub. This will keep in a covered bottle in the refrigerator for up to 6 weeks

◆ To prepare the chicken, mix 2 tablespoons spice rub with the olive oil, chives and garlic. Rub chicken pieces all over with the marinade and leave for about 1 hour.

◆ Preheat oven to 400°F.

◆ Place chicken pieces on a baking sheet and roast for about 30 minutes until done.

Serves 4–6

Chicken stew with olives and garlic

1 tbs minced chives

1 tbs chopped thyme

6 cloves garlic, chopped

2 tbs vegetable oil

3 lb chicken, cut in half

1 cup canned whole tomatoes with juice, crushed

¼ cup olives, sliced

¼ cup chicken stock

¼ cup rum

Meat

◆ Combine in a small mixing bowl the minced chives, thyme and half the garlic. Season with salt and freshly ground black pepper, add 1 tablespoon of the oil and combine to make a paste.

◆ Rub paste onto chicken, stuffing some under the skin. Cover and refrigerate for 1 hour.

◆ Heat the remaining oil in a sauté pan, add chicken and brown, turning to ensure even browning. Add the tomatoes, the rest of the garlic and the olives. Bring to the boil, cover and simmer for about 10 minutes, basting frequently with the pan juices and adding a little chicken stock if necessary to prevent sticking.

◆ After 10 minutes turn chicken over and continue cooking until chicken is tender.

◆ Remove chicken to a platter, and place sauce in a shallow frying pan. Heat and add rum, flambé and pour over chicken in platter. Serve warm.

Serves 4

Coconut curried chicken with lemongrass

4 chicken breasts, boned and cut into cubes

3 cloves garlic, minced

1 tbs rum (optional)

2 tbs vegetable oil

1 onion, chopped

2 tbs sliced lemongrass

1 tbs minced ginger

1 tbs curry powder

½ cup coconut milk

2 tsp sesame oil

1 bell pepper, seeded and chopped

1 carrot, chopped

◆ Rub the chicken with the garlic and rum, if using. Let sit for 15 minutes.

◆ Heat oil in a sauté pan, add onion and cook until tender. Add lemongrass and ginger and cook for about 2 minutes more. Add chicken and cook for 5 minutes until it loses its color.

◆ Combine the curry powder with the coconut milk and sesame oil.

◆ Add bell pepper and carrot to chicken, and cook for 2 minutes longer. Add the coconut milk mixture and bring to the boil. Season with salt and freshly ground black pepper. Lower heat and simmer for 10 minutes.

◆ Taste and adjust seasonings before serving.

Serves 4–6

Creamy pasta and pesto chicken

A taste of the Mediterranean, this dish is alive with flavor!

1 lb boneless chicken breasts

1 tbs pesto sauce or ground fresh basil

2 cloves garlic, minced

2 tbs olive oil

½ tsp freshly ground black pepper

1 onion, finely chopped

2 tbs all-purpose flour

1 cup milk

1 cup chicken stock

1 cup sliced mushrooms

1 red bell pepper, seeded and cut into strips

¼ cup dry sherry (optional)

1 lb spaghetti

Parmesan cheese (optional)

¼ cup finely chopped basil or parsley

◆ Cut chicken into thin strips.

◆ Combine pesto, garlic and 1 tablespoon olive oil. Combine the chicken strips with the pesto marinade and sprinkle with the black pepper. Let marinate in the refrigerator for 30 minutes.

◆ Heat remaining olive oil in a sauté pan, add onion and sweat for a couple of minutes until tender and fragrant. Add chicken and cook until it loses its pinkness, about 4–5 minutes.

◆ Sprinkle on the flour and stir to combine. Add milk and stock and cook until bubbly and mixture thickens. Stir constantly at this stage. Add the mushrooms, pepper and sherry, if using. Stir and cook for a couple of minutes more. Season with salt and pepper to taste. Remove from heat.

◆ Boil pasta according to package directions. Drain and place in a large shallow bowl.

◆ Gently reheat chicken and sauce. Pour over pasta and toss to combine.

◆ Serve with a sprinkling of grated Parmesan cheese if desired. Garnish with chopped basil or parsley.

Serves 4–6

Meat

Sunshine brochettes

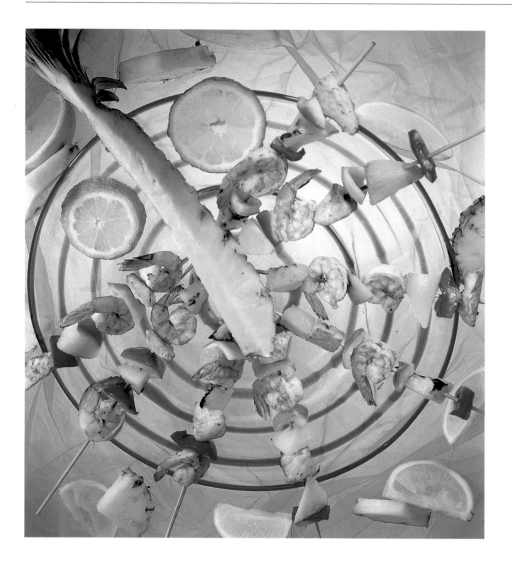

12 large shrimp

$\frac{1}{2}$ lb boneless chicken, cut into $\frac{1}{2}$ inch pieces

1 onion, cut into quarters

1 bell pepper, seeded and cut into 1 inch pieces

12 fresh pineapple chunks

2 tbs minced chives

2 cloves garlic, minced

2 tbs red wine vinegar

4 tbs vegetable oil

salt and freshly ground black pepper

12 wooden skewers, soaked in water overnight

◆ Combine all the ingredients and marinate for about 30 minutes.

◆ Preheat broiler or grill.

◆ Thread shrimp, chicken, vegetables and fruit onto the skewers. Place on greased baking tray and broil for 6–8 minutes, turning twice, until charred and cooked.

Serves 6

Cheese-stuffed burgers

1 lb lean ground beef or chicken

1 tbs minced chives

2 tsp chopped thyme

1 tbs chopped basil

2 cloves garlic, minced

¼ cup breadcrumbs

1 egg, beaten

4 tbs feta cheese or other cheese

◆ Combine beef or chicken with the herbs. Add garlic, breadcrumbs and beaten egg. Season with salt and freshly ground black pepper. Mix well.

◆ Divide mixture into 4 portions. Roll each portion into a ball, then make a small indentation in each ball and place about 1 tablespoon of cheese into the center of each. Close the indentation, bringing the meat around. Flatten each patty to about ¾–1 inch thickness.

◆ Cook on greased grill over hot coals turning once, for about 10–12 minutes or until desired doneness. Or the patties may be broiled, grilled or pan fried on your stove for about 4 minutes each side.

Makes 4

Beef with vegetables and noodles

½ lb egg noodles

12 oz beef, sliced into ¼ inch thin slices

4 tbs vegetable oil

⅔ lb mixed vegetables, cut into 1½ inch pieces

For the marinade

2 tbs soy sauce

1 tbs rum (optional)

2 tsp minced garlic

1 tsp sesame oil

1 tsp cornstarch

For the sauce

1 cup chicken stock

¼ cup oyster sauce

1 tbs soy sauce

2 tsp sugar

1 tsp sesame oil

1 tbs cornstarch

4 tbs vegetable oil

Seasonings

3 tbs minced chives

1 tbs minced ginger

1 tbs minced garlic

Meat

◆ Cook the noodles until tender according to manufacturer's directions. Drain and set aside.

◆ Combine marinade ingredients, and mix with beef. Marinate for about 1 hour or overnight.

◆ Combine the sauce ingredients and set aside.

◆ Heat a wok and add 2 tablespoons of oil. Add the beef and stirfry until it loses its pinkness. Remove.

◆ Clean pan, heat 1 tablespoon of oil and add seasonings. Stirfry until fragrant. Add the vegetables and cover to steam for a few minutes. Add sauce and stir well until thick. Add beef slices, toss to coat and remove from heat.

◆ Heat a large frying pan, add remaining oil. When hot add noodles and press into pan to form a solid mass. Flip the noodle cake and brown on the other side.

◆ Remove from heat to a serving platter, spoon the beef and vegetables over the cake and serve.

Serves 4

Beef curry

2 lb boneless beef, cut into 1 inch chunks

2 tbs minced garlic

1 tbs minced thyme

2 tbs minced chives

4 tbs vegetable oil

2 onions, thinly sliced

4 tbs curry powder

¼ cup water

2 cups coconut milk

1 Congo pepper or hot pepper, left whole

2 tbs chopped chadon beni (cilantro)

◆ Season beef with garlic, thyme and chives.

◆ Heat oil in a large sauté pan and cook onions until almost browned.

◆ Dissolve curry powder in the water, add to hot oil and cook until thick and almost dry. Add beef and stir to coat beef pieces evenly.

◆ Add about ⅓ cup of coconut milk and lower heat. Drop in hot pepper, cover. Add the rest of the coconut milk gradually, until the beef is cooked and tender, 35–40 minutes. Remove the hot pepper.

◆ Sprinkle the chadon beni over the beef and serve.

Serves 4–6

Meat

Honey barbecued lamb shoulder chops

8 lamb shoulder or loin chops, sliced 1 inch thick

zesty barbecue sauce (see page 195)

For the marinade

6 cloves garlic, minced

2 tbs honey

2 tbs soy sauce

2 tbs minced fresh herbs (thyme, basil, chives, etc.)

1 tbs lemon juice or red wine vinegar

1 tsp freshly ground black pepper

◆ Combine all the ingredients for the marinade and rub onto the chops. Marinate for 4 hours or overnight.

◆ Cook lamb on greased grill over medium hot setting, turning once, for 5–6 minutes per side or until desired doneness. Baste with zesty barbecue sauce while cooking.

Serves 4

Grilled marinated oriental lamb

3 lb lamb shoulder chops or boneless lamb, about 1–1½ inches thick

For the marinade

¼ cup hoisin sauce

1 tbs Chinese chili sauce

1 tbs tomato ketchup

2 tbs brown sugar

1 tsp sesame oil

2 tbs soy sauce

4 cloves garlic, minced

1 tbs minced ginger

1 tsp freshly ground black pepper

◆ Combine all the marinade ingredients in a mixing bowl. Rub mixture onto the lamb pieces. Cover and marinate for 4 hours.

◆ Preheat grill or broiler and cook chops for about 6 minutes per side.

Serves 4–6

Meat

Caribbean lamb stew

This classic stew uses the old African method of caramelizing sugar to give the meat a rich brown color.

6 lamb shoulder slices, about 1 inch thick

2 tbs olive or vegetable oil

2 tbs brown sugar

2 onions, thinly sliced

8 cloves garlic, minced

2 pimento peppers, seeded and chopped

½ hot pepper, seeded and chopped

1 cup canned whole tomatoes, crushed with juice

For the marinade

2 tbs minced chives

2 tbs fresh thyme

2 cloves garlic, minced

1 tsp freshly ground black pepper

◆ Combine all the ingredients for the marinade.

◆ Cut lamb slices in 2 inch pieces and marinate for 2 hours or overnight.

◆ Heat oil in a large skillet, add sugar and let caramelize. It will get very frothy, then turn a rich caramel color. Add the lamb at this point. Be careful, as it will spit and sputter, so a splatter shield is a good idea here. Brown the lamb pieces on both sides until meat is nicely browned. Add the onions, garlic and peppers and sauté until fragrant, about 4 minutes. Add the tomatoes.

◆ Cover and simmer for 1 hour or more, adding a little water if necessary to prevent sticking, until the meat is tender.

◆ Taste and season with salt and freshly ground black pepper.

Serves 6

Meat

Caribbean lamb stew with Cornmeal coo-coo (page 118)

Meat

Hot and spicy chili with lamb and black beans

Traditional chili con carne is a favorite in the Caribbean. Ground lamb and black beans marry well in this hearty and nourishing chili, which is a delightful twist on the old favorite. The chipolte chili adds a marvellous smoky and hot flavor to this dish – if you can't find it, just omit it.

2 tbs vegetable oil

1 lb ground lamb

4 cloves garlic, minced

½ cup chopped chives

2 large onions, cut into large pieces

2 tbs good quality chili powder

1 tbs ground roasted cumin (geera)

1 can (14 oz) black beans

1 can (14 oz) whole tomatoes with juice

1 Congo pepper, roasted and seeded

1 tsp salt, or to taste

1 chipolte chili in adobe sauce (optional)

¼ cup chopped chadon beni (cilantro)

◆ Heat the oil in a large heavy skillet. Add the lamb and brown until fat runs off. Remove from heat and pour off fat. Return to heat and add garlic and chives. Stir to combine. Add onions, chili powder and cumin. Continue cooking for about 2 minutes.

◆ Add black beans, tomatoes, Congo pepper, salt and chipolte chili, if using. Cook until chili begins to bubble. Cover and simmer for about 30–40 minutes.

◆ Sprinkle chadon beni over just before serving. Serve with sizzling corn bread (see page 185).

Serves 6

Meat

Roast leg of lamb

Roasted lamb is a favorite on the islands, especially for Easter.

8 cloves garlic, minced

2 tbs Dijon mustard

2 tsp coarsely cracked black pepper

2 tbs red wine vinegar

2 tbs olive oil

2 tbs chopped fresh rosemary

4–5 lb leg of lamb, bone in

◆ In a food processor combine the garlic, mustard, pepper, red wine vinegar, oil and rosemary. Process until thoroughly mixed. Rub marinade over lamb and marinate overnight in the refrigerator.

◆ Preheat oven to 400°F.

◆ Roast lamb for 1–1¼ hours or until desired texture is reached. Allow roast to rest for 15 minutes before carving.

Serves 6–8

Coconut curried goat

2 lb lean goat meat, cut into ½ inch cubes

2 tbs minced chives

2 tbs natural yogurt

4 cloves garlic, minced

1 tbs dark rum

4 tbs good quality curry powder

2 tbs vegetable oil

1 onion, finely chopped

2 Congo peppers, seeded and chopped

2 pimento peppers, seeded and chopped

1 tbs grated ginger

1 tbs minced thyme

1 tsp salt

1 cup coconut milk, preferably fresh

2 tbs chadon beni (cilantro), finely chopped

◆ Marinate the goat meat in the minced chives, yogurt, half the minced garlic, rum and 2 tablespoons of the curry powder. Leave overnight.

◆ Heat the oil in a large iron pot. Add the remaing garlic, onion, peppers, ginger and thyme. Sauté for about 4 minutes.

◆ Mix the rest of the curry powder with 4 tablespoons of water. Add to pot and cook until the water has dried. Add goat meat and brown, stirring occasionally.

◆ Add salt and cover, adding a small amount of coconut milk to prevent sticking. Cook until tender, about 1 hour, adding more coconut milk as needed to prevent sticking.

◆ Taste and adjust salt. Add chadon beni and remove from heat.

Serves 4

Meat

Seafood flavors

When one thinks of Caribbean food one immediately thinks of seafood. Here, you are usually only a few minutes away from the water and so there is the great advantage of enjoying today's catch today. Freshly caught seafood is not a novelty or scarcity on the islands, it's a way of life. The price of fish will vary with the weather, type of fish and time of year but generally it is cheap enough for everyone to afford.

The beauty of consuming freshly caught fish is that the delicious flavor of the fish really shines through when you're eating it, and you don't need a lot of flavor enhancers to heighten the taste.

The more popular types of fish are flying fish – which has become a national emblem of Barbados – shark, grouper, kingfish, dolphin, snapper, white salmon and carite.

Fish is cooked in many ways in the Caribbean: stuffed and baked (Baked stuffed carite); filleted, breaded and fried (Fisherman's fried fish); sautéed with aromatics (Creole fish fillets with pimento and thyme); grilled, and fried in a cornmeal batter (Cornmeal-crusted flying fish). These are all great ways to enjoy fish.

The more popular shellfish used are shrimp, crab and lobster. Shrimp is prepared in many ways, from grilling to currying. Lobster is a scarcity in most homes due to the prohibitive prices but can be found on most restaurant menus through the islands. Crab is a main ingredient in callaloo, but is also worth trying in Tobago curried crab with dumplings.

Preserved fish is also quite popular on the islands. Dating back to the days when there was no refrigeration, drying, salting and smoking fish were the only ways of preserving. These preserved fish are still available today. Dried salted cod is the main ingredient in Trinidad and Tobago's saltfish bull jhol; smoked herring is delicious in smoked herring bull jhol; and salted cod is also the star of accras, a salted codfish fritter, known in the French Caribbean and in Trinidad and Tobago by that name, and in Jamaica as 'stamp and go'.

Caribbean shrimp curry

2 lb medium shrimp, peeled and deveined

2 cloves garlic, minced

1 tsp freshly ground black pepper

1 tsp salt

1 tbs vegetable oil

4 tsp curry powder mixed with ¼ cup water

1 tbs minced chives

1 tbs minced ginger

1 hot pepper, seeded and chopped

1 pimento pepper, seeded and chopped

1 bell pepper, seeded and chopped

2 tomatoes, chopped

¼ cup rum (optional)

½ cup chicken stock

◆ Marinate shrimp in half the minced garlic, the black pepper and ½ teaspoon salt.

◆ Heat the oil in a sauté pan, add remaining garlic and curry paste and stir until sizzling. Add chives, ginger and peppers and cook for 2 minutes longer. Add tomatoes, rum, if using, and chicken stock. Add remaining salt. Cover and simmer for about 10 minutes. The mixture should be reduced to about a half.

◆ Add shrimp and cook gently until shrimp just begin to curl, about 5 minutes.

◆ Serve hot with steaming hot jasmine rice.

Serves 4

Grilled shrimp with lime and garlic

⅓ cup fresh lime juice

2 tsp grated lime zest

⅓ cup vegetable or olive oil

¼ cup finely chopped parsley or chadon beni (cilantro)

4 cloves garlic, minced

1 tbs dark rum

freshly ground black pepper

24 large shrimp, peeled and deveined

◆ In a mixing bowl combine the lime juice and zest, oil, parsley, garlic, rum and pepper. Place shrimp in marinade and toss. Cover and refrigerate for 30 minutes.

◆ Thread shrimp onto a metal skewer or a wooden skewer that has been soaked in water for 30 minutes.

◆ Cook shrimp on greased grill over medium hot coals or grill, brushing often with the marinade. Cook for 2 minutes per side or until firm to the touch.

Serves 4

Baked stuffed carite

Carite is a tender, flavorful fish, much like snapper but with less bones!

2 tbs minced chives	2 pimento peppers, seeded and finely chopped
3 cloves garlic, minced	1/2 cup finely chopped chives
1 tbs olive oil	1 tsp minced garlic
3 1/2 lb whole carite or snapper	1 tbs fresh thyme
For the stuffing	1/2 lb shrimp, peeled and chopped
4 oz butter plus 2 tbs	1/2–1 cup fine breadcrumbs
1/2 cup finely chopped onions	1 egg
1/2 cup finely chopped sweet pepper	1/4 cup grated Parmesan cheese

◆ Combine the chives with the garlic and olive oil. Rub mixture over fish and sprinkle with salt and freshly ground black pepper.

◆ Preheat oven to 350°F.

◆ Make the stuffing. Melt 4 oz butter in a large sauté pan and add onions, pepper, pimentos, chives, garlic and thyme. Sauté until fragrant. Add shrimp and sauté for about 30 seconds.

◆ Add about 1/2 cup breadcrumbs and cook until mixture sticks to the bottom of the pan. Add remaining butter. Scrape the mixture from the pan continuously.

◆ Combine the egg with the cheese. Add to mixture, stir and cool.

◆ Stuff fish with the stuffing, closing the cavity with metal skewers. Place the fish in foil and tent.

◆ Bake for about 45 minutes until fish is cooked.

Serves 4–6

Seafood

Broiled lobster with cilantro lime butter

⅓ cup butter

2 cloves garlic, minced

1 tsp chopped hot pepper (optional)

1 tbs fresh lime juice

1 tbs finely chopped chadon beni (cilantro)

salt and freshly ground black pepper

2 lobsters, live or frozen

◆ Melt the butter in a small saucepan. Add the garlic and pepper, if using. Cook to a sizzle until fragrant, taking care not to burn or brown the garlic. Remove from heat and stir in all the remaining ingredients except the lobster.

◆ Heat 3 quarts of water in a large pot. Add 2 tablespoons salt and bring water to the boil. Plunge lobsters into water, head first. Cover and heat to boiling, then reduce heat and cook for a further 10–15 minutes. Remove lobsters and drain.

◆ Preheat broiler.

◆ Place lobsters on their backs. Cut into halves, lengthways, with a sharp knife. Remove stomach, which is just behind the head, and remove the intestinal vein which runs from the tip of the tail to the stomach. Crack the claws.

◆ Place tails meat side up on a baking pan, drizzle with some of the cilantro butter. Broil 3 inches from heat until hot, 2–3 minutes. Remove and serve with remaining cilantro lime butter.

Serves 2–3

Seafood

Broiled lobster with cilantro lime butter

French Caribbean shrimp sauté

1½ lb medium shrimp, peeled and deveined

2 cloves garlic, minced

2 tbs olive oil

½ Congo pepper, seeded and chopped

3 ripe medium tomatoes, chopped

½ cup chopped chives

1 tbs fresh French thyme

¼ cup golden rum (optional)

½ cup chopped basil

◆ Sprinkle shrimp with salt and freshly ground black pepper, add ½ teaspoon minced garlic, combine and let marinate for 15 minutes.

◆ Heat oil in a sauté pan, add remaining garlic and the pepper and heat to fragrant. Add tomatoes, chives and thyme, and sauté for about 2–4 minutes until tomatoes begin to soften. Drop in the shrimp and sauté until pink and curled.

◆ If using rum, tilt the pan towards the flame, pour the rum over and flambé.

◆ Turn out onto a platter and sprinkle with fresh basil.

Serves 4

Spicy grilled shrimp with bulgur wheat pilaf

1 tbs vegetable oil

2 cloves garlic, chopped

1 onion, chopped

2 cups assorted fresh vegetables, cut into 1 inch pieces

1 cup bulgur wheat

1¼ cups vegetable or chicken stock

1 lb shrimp combined with 1 tsp minced garlic and 1 tbs minced chives

2 tbs chopped mint

2 tsp hot chili oil (optional)

◆ Heat a medium sauté pan and add the vegetable oil. Add garlic and onion and sauté until fragrant.

◆ Add vegetables and toss to combine. Add bulgur wheat, salt to taste and the stock. Bring to the boil, cover and simmer for 10 minutes until tender. Fluff with a fork.

◆ Preheat broiler or grill.

◆ Place marinated shrimp on a baking sheet or into a shallow dish. Broil for 3 minutes per side.

◆ Remove and serve with the wheat pilaf. Sprinkle with chopped mint and drizzle with hot chili oil if desired.

Serves 4

Seafood

Coconut fish with lemongrass and hot peppers

1 lb fresh fish fillets (carite or kingfish), cut into 4 portions

1 tbs minced chives plus 2 tbs fresh chives, white and green parts, finely chopped

salt and freshly ground black pepper

1 tbs vegetable oil

2 cloves garlic, minced

1 onion, chopped

1 red Congo pepper, seeded and cut into strips

2 stalks fresh lemongrass, thinly sliced

2 tomatoes, seeded and chopped

$3/4$ cup coconut milk

$1/2$ tsp fresh lime juice

◆ Clean and wash fish fillets. Season lightly with minced chives, salt and black pepper.

◆ Heat the oil in a medium sauté pan and add garlic, onion, chopped chives, hot pepper and lemongrass. Sauté until fragrant, about 1 minute, then add the tomatoes. Add coconut milk to pan and bring to the boil. Reduce heat and simmer for about 10 minutes.

◆ Season to taste. Purée sauce in a blender and strain, then return sauce to pan.

◆ Add fish fillets and cook for about 4 minutes on each side, basting frequently with the sauce.

◆ Remove from heat, adjust seasonings, sprinkle on lime juice and serve immediately.

Serves 2–3

Grilled marinated carite with fresh tomato coriander salsa

1 tsp vegetable oil

1 tbs minced chives

2 cloves garlic, minced

1 tsp ground coriander

4 carite fillets (5–6 oz each), or any other fresh fish

1 tbs chopped coriander (optional)

For the salsa

3 ripe tomatoes

½ green hot pepper, seeded and chopped

1½ tsp fresh lime juice

1 large clove garlic, minced

2 tsp olive oil

1½ tbs ground coriander

½ tsp salt

1 tsp freshly ground black pepper

¼ cup finely chopped chadon beni (cilantro)

◆ About half an hour before cooking mix the vegetable oil with the minced chives and garlic. Stir in the ground coriander and add salt and freshly ground black pepper.

◆ Wash fish and pat dry. Spread marinade over both sides, cover and refrigerate.

◆ Meanwhile, make the salsa. Peel, seed and chop the tomatoes. Add the hot pepper, lime juice, garlic, oil and ground coriander. Season with the salt and pepper and set aside. Add the chadon beni just before serving.

◆ Preheat broiler, and broil carite fillets for about 3–5 minutes on each side.

◆ Serve the fish topped with the salsa. Sprinkle with fresh coriander if desired.

Serves 4

Cornmeal-coated fish fingers with cilantro dip

2 tbs ground chives

1 tbs minced garlic

1 tbs olive oil

3 lb firm fish fillets, cut into 1 inch by 3 inch pieces

1 cup flour

1 cup yellow cornmeal

2 tbs ground roasted cumin (geera)

2 tsp salt

2 tsp black pepper

2 tsp cayenne pepper

2 eggs

oil for frying

For the dip

1 cup low-fat yogurt

1 cup low-fat mayonnaise

1 cup chopped chadon beni (cilantro)

1/2 cup chopped chives

1/2 tbs horseradish sauce

1 tbs ketchup

1 Congo or hot pepper, seeded and chopped

salt

◆ Combine all the ingredients for the dip and refrigerate until needed.

◆ Combine the ground chives with the garlic and olive oil. Rub mixture gently over fish fingers.

◆ In a flat dish combine the flour with the cornmeal, cumin, salt, pepper and cayenne.

◆ Beat the eggs in another flat dish.

◆ Dip fish fingers first into flour mixture, then into beaten eggs. Then dip into flour mixture again.

◆ Heat oil in a large frying pan, fry fingers, turning once, for about 2–3 minutes per side. Serve warm with the cilantro dip.

Makes about 30

Seafood

Spicy Caribbean fish cakes

1 lb fish fillets, steamed

½ cup soft breadcrumbs

½ cup finely chopped mixed herbs (parsley, thyme, basil, chives)

salt and freshly ground black pepper

1 tsp Dijon mustard

2 tsp hot pepper sauce

½ tsp fresh lime juice

1 egg, lightly beaten

1 cup dried breadcrumbs

oil for frying

◆ Flake fish and remove any bones. Add soft breadcrumbs, herbs, salt and pepper, mustard, pepper sauce, lime juice and egg.

◆ Form into cakes about 1½–2 inches in diameter.

◆ Place dried crumbs on a plate. Dip cakes into crumbs and cover on both sides.

◆ Fry in hot oil, until golden on both sides.

Makes 12

Oven-baked fishy fingers

6 oz fresh fish fillets

2 cloves garlic, minced

½ tsp salt

2 tsp minced chives

½ cup fresh breadcrumbs

¼ cup grated Parmesan cheese

1 egg, lightly beaten

◆ Cut the fish into 3 inch by 1 inch strips.

◆ Combine the garlic, salt and chives. Rub chive mixture onto the fish fingers.

◆ In a separate bowl combine breadcrumbs with cheese.

◆ Dip fish into beaten egg, then roll in crumb and cheese mixture. Repeat until all the fingers have been coated with crumbs. Place in the refrigerator on a plate.

◆ Preheat oven to 375°F.

◆ Place fish fingers on baking sheet and bake for about 5 minutes on each side, until fish is nicely browned and crusty. Remove and serve warm.

Makes about 8

Pepper shrimp

This makes a great starter.

12 large shrimp, cleaned and deveined

1 tbs minced garlic

½ tsp salt

4 tbs cornstarch or potato starch

1 egg white

vegetable oil for frying

1 Congo or hot pepper, seeded and chopped

1 tbs Chinese chili garlic sauce

½ tbs oyster sauce

1 tbs tomato ketchup

½ tsp granulated sugar

½ tsp Worcestershire sauce

1 tsp sesame oil

¼ cup chopped chives

◆ Marinate the shrimp in the garlic and salt for 10 minutes.

◆ Combine cornstarch with egg white to make a batter. Add a little water if necessary.

◆ Heat a wok and add about ½ cup vegetable oil.

◆ Dip shrimp into batter, place pieces into hot oil and fry until golden. Drain.

◆ Clean wok and add about 1 tablespoon vegetable oil. Add hot pepper and chili garlic sauce, and stirfry until fragrant. Add the rest of the ingredients, except for the shrimp and chives, and stirfry until combined. Add shrimp and toss until all the shrimp are coated with sauce.

◆ Sprinkle with chives, remove shrimp from pan and serve.

Makes 12

Seafood

Tobago curried crab with dumplings

This Tobago specialty is a must try!

3 tbs curry powder

½ cup water

6 blue crabs, or other, cleaned

salt and freshly ground black pepper

4 cloves garlic, chopped

juice of 1 lime

2 tbs vegetable oil

1 onion, chopped

1 hot pepper, seeded and chopped

4 cups coconut milk

¼ cup chopped chives

¼ cup chopped chadon beni (cilantro)

dumplings (see page 31)

◆ Combine the curry powder with the water.

◆ Season crabs with salt, pepper, half the garlic and the lime juice. Let stand for 30 minutes.

◆ Heat the oil in a large sauté pan. Add remaining garlic, onion and hot pepper. Cook for about 1 minute, then add curry mixture and cook until thick. Add crabs and stir to let curry mixture cover crabs in the pot.

◆ Add coconut milk and sprinkle on chives and chadon beni. Cook until bubbly, cover and simmer, stirring occasionally, for about 20–30 minutes.

◆ Drop dumplings into crab mixture, cover and steam for a further 10 minutes, turning dumplings once. If mixture seems too dry add a little more coconut milk or water.

◆ Taste and adjust seasonings. Sprinkle on more chadon beni if desired.

Serves 4–6

Seafood

Tobago curried crab with dumplings

Caribbean fish bull jhol

1 lb fresh fish fillets

1 tsp minced chives

salt and freshly ground black pepper

1 tsp minced garlic

3 tbs olive oil

1 large onion, thinly sliced

1 pimento pepper, seeded and chopped

1 large tomato, chopped

lettuce leaves

2 eggs, hard boiled

2 tbs chopped chadon beni (cilantro)

◆ Preheat broiler.

◆ Marinate fish in chives, salt, black pepper, garlic and 1 tablespoon olive oil.

◆ Place in heatproof platter and broil for 4 minutes per side. Remove and flake gently with a fork. Place in a large bowl.

◆ Heat remaining oil in a non-stick sauté pan, and sauté onion and pepper for only 1 minute.

◆ Remove, and add to fish. Add tomato, and toss. Season with salt if needed.

◆ Place fish mixture onto platter, decorate with lettuce and egg wedges. Season with salt and pepper. Sprinkle on chadon beni.

Serves 4–6

Fisherman's fried fish

2 lb fresh fish fillets, cut into 8 pieces

1 tbs minced chives

½ tbs minced celery

½ tbs thyme

4 cloves garlic, minced

1 tbs lime juice

1 tbs olive oil

1 tsp salt

1 tsp freshly ground black pepper

1 cup fine breadcrumbs

1 egg, lightly beaten

vegetable oil for frying

◆ Wash fish. Combine chives, celery, thyme, garlic, lime juice, olive oil, salt and pepper. Rub marinade over fish and let marinate for 20 minutes.

◆ Place breadcrumbs on a plate and season with salt.

◆ Dip fish first into beaten egg, then into crumb mixture. Shallow fry fish for about 3 minutes per side until golden. Remove and drain.

◆ Serve with rice and peas and a fresh salad.

Serves 4–6

Seafood

Pan-fried snapper with mushroom, pepper and Parmesan stuffing

3 tbs vegetable oil

1 tsp minced garlic

1 tsp minced chives

½ tsp salt

2 whole snapper, 1½ lb each, cleaned

½ cup seasoned flour

For the stuffing

1 tbs vegetable oil

½ onion, chopped

1 tbs chopped chives

1 tsp minced garlic

¼ cup chopped sweet red pepper

2 large dried black mushrooms, soaked in warm water for 1 hour, drained and chopped (reserve water)

½ cup fresh breadcrumbs

salt and freshly ground black pepper

⅓ cup chopped parsley

⅓ cup grated Parmesan cheese

◆ Combine 1 tablespoon oil with the garlic, chives, salt and some freshly ground black pepper. Rub onto snapper and let marinate for 20 minutes.

◆ Make the stuffing. Heat the vegetable oil in a sauté pan. Add the onion, chives, garlic, pepper and mushrooms. Sauté for 5 minutes, add breadcrumbs, salt, pepper and parsley. Add cheese and 1 tablespoon mushroom water. Stir to bring stuffing together (add more water if necessary), taste and adjust seasonings. Cool.

◆ Stuff snapper with stuffing. Hold cavity together with toothpicks or small skewers.

◆ Dredge snappers in seasoned flour.

◆ Heat remaining oil in a large frying pan, and pan fry snapper on both sides until lightly browned. Cover and add about 1 tablespoon of water to prevent sticking. Continue cooking on a low heat for 15–20 minutes, turning once, until fish is cooked.

Serves 2–3

Herbed fish steaks

1/4 cup minced fresh herbs (basil, chives, parsley or chadon beni)

2 tbs fresh lime juice

1/4 cup olive oil

2 cloves garlic, minced

2 tsp Dijon mustard

freshly ground black pepper

1 1/2 lb kingfish or shark steak, sliced 3/4 inch thick

◆ In a shallow dish large enough to hold the fish in a single layer mix together the herbs, lime juice, oil, garlic, mustard and pepper. Add fish steaks and turn to coat evenly. Cover and let marinate for 30 minutes at room temperature.

◆ Cook on greased grill over hot coals or on high setting for 3–4 minutes on each side, until cooked, brushing frequently with marinade. Season with salt.

Serves 4

Smoked herring bull jhol

Serve this with fried bakes or coconut bake (see pages 188 and 186).

6 oz smoked herring

1/2 lime

2 tbs olive oil

1 large onion, chopped

3 tomatoes, chopped

1 sweet pepper, seeded and sliced

1/2 Congo or hot pepper, seeded and chopped

6 lettuce leaves

2 eggs, hard boiled and cut into quarters

1 avocado, sliced

◆ To prepare herring, place in a large bowl, cover with boiling water and squeeze the juice from 1/2 lime into it. Let soak for 30 minutes. Drain and repeat once again, if necessary. The soaking should remove any excess oil from the herring and some salt. Remove from water, drain and squeeze herring to remove excess water. Remove bones.

◆ Heat the oil in a frying pan. Add onions, tomatoes and peppers, and stir. Add herring and toss to combine. Remove from heat.

◆ Arrange lettuce on a platter, place smoked herring mixture in the centre, garnish with boiled eggs and avocado. Sprinkle with freshly ground black pepper.

Serves 4–6

Seafood

Herbed fish steaks with Dasheen salad (page 116)

Shrimp sauté with basil and feta

A taste of the Mediterranean, basil grows quite well in the Caribbean and seems to be appearing more in recipes of the region. If wished, Parmesan cheese could be used instead of feta.

1lb linguini pasta

3 tbs olive oil

1½ lb medium shrimp, peeled and deveined

salt and freshly ground black pepper

4 cloves garlic, chopped

1 small onion, chopped finely

3 ripe medium tomatoes, chopped

½ cup chopped basil

feta cheese for garnishing

◆ Boil pasta, according to package instructions, and drain. Add 1 tablespoon olive oil and toss. Keep warm.

◆ Sprinkle shrimp with salt, pepper and ½ teaspoon chopped garlic.

◆ Heat remaining oil in sauté pan, add remaining garlic and onion. Heat to fragrant. Add tomatoes and basil, and sauté for about 2–4 minutes until tomatoes begin to soften. If mixture begins to dry add a little stock or water. Season with salt and pepper.

◆ Drop in shrimp and sauté until pink and curled, about 2–3 minutes per side.

◆ Serve shrimp on top of a bed of pasta. Sprinkle with feta cheese and more black pepper if needed.

Serves 2–4

Saltfish bull jhol

Bull jhol is a local term for our traditional saltfish and vegetable salad, which is served at many a local Sunday brunch or breakfast. It is served with either fried bakes or roast coconut bake. First the saltfish is soaked, then combined with a delicious combination of peppers, onions and tomatoes and served with avocado (when in season), lettuce and sliced hard boiled eggs.

½ lb boneless, salted cod

juice of ½ lime

¼ cup olive oil

2 large onions, finely chopped

2 large tomatoes, chopped

½ hot pepper, seeded and chopped (Congo or habanero)

1 bell pepper, seeded and chopped

¼ cup chopped parsley or chadon beni (cilantro)

8 lettuce leaves

1 avocado (if available)

2 eggs, hard boiled and sliced

Seafood

Saltfish bull jhol with Fried bakes (page 188)

◆ Cut saltfish into 1 inch chunks and soak overnight in cool water, changing the water about 3 times.

◆ Wash fish and flake, tasting to ensure enough salt has been removed. Drain fish and add lime juice.

◆ Heat 2 tablespoons olive oil in a sauté pan, add onions and sauté for about 30 seconds. Add fish and toss to combine quickly.

Remove, and combine onions and fish with tomatoes, hot pepper and bell pepper. Toss to mix. Add the remaining olive oil and season with salt and freshly ground black pepper.

◆ Place saltfish bull jhol on a serving platter and sprinkle with parsley. Surround fish with lettuce, sliced avocado and sliced eggs.

Serves 4–6

Seafood

Creole fish fillets with pimento and thyme

2 tbs minced thyme

2 tbs minced chives

salt and freshly ground black pepper

1 clove garlic, minced

2 lb firm fish fillets (kingfish, carite or salmon)

2 tbs olive oil

1 small onion, chopped

1 pimento pepper, seeded and chopped

½ hot pepper, seeded and chopped (optional)

2 small tomatoes, seeded and chopped

◆ In a small bowl combine the thyme, chives, salt, pepper and garlic. Rub marinade onto fish fillets and let marinate for 30 minutes.

◆ Heat the oil in a sauté pan, add onion and peppers, and sauté until onions are tender, 10–15 minutes. Add tomatoes and continue cooking until tomatoes are almost saucy, adding just a little water to prevent sticking, about 4–5 minutes.

◆ Add fish fillets and baste with sauce. Cook for about 3–5 minutes per side. Season with salt and pepper and remove from heat.

Serves 4

Grilled fish fillets with herbed butter

1½ lb firm fish fillets, cut into 1 inch thick slices (kingfish or grouper is a good option here)

For the marinade

2 tbs minced chives

½ tbs thyme

½ tbs minced celery

1 tbs lime juice

4 cloves garlic, minced

2 tbs olive oil

For the butter

¼ cup olive oil

¼ cup butter

1 tsp thyme

2 tbs parsley

2 cloves garlic, minced

1 tbs chopped basil

1 tsp freshly ground black pepper

◆ Combine all the ingredients for the butter in a blender. Refrigerate until ready for use.

◆ Combine all the ingredients for the marinade in a blender or food processor. Rub marinade over fish fillets. Refrigerate for about 20 minutes.

◆ Preheat grill, broiler or barbecue. Grease grill and grill fish for about 3–4 minutes per side. Serve with the herbed butter.

Serves 4

Seafood

Cornmeal-crusted flying fish *with island tartar sauce*

Flying fish is a Bajan specialty – they call their island 'Land of the flying fish'!
Here is a delightful twist on a traditional recipe.

Cornmeal-crusted flying fish and Sweet potato French fries (page 119)

2 tbs minced chives	1 tbs lime juice	*For the batter*
1 tsp minced thyme	6 flying fish fillets	3/4 cup all-purpose flour
1 tsp minced garlic	1/4 cup flour	1 large egg
1 tsp salt	1 cup cornmeal	1/2 cup beer (or milk or water)
1 tsp freshly ground black pepper	vegetable oil for frying	salt and freshly ground black pepper

Seafood

◆ Combine the herbs, garlic, salt and pepper with the lime juice. Rub onto fish fillets and let stand, covered, for 15 minutes.

◆ Combine all the batter ingredients to make a smooth batter. If batter seems too thick, thin with more liquid.

◆ Place flour and cornmeal on two separate plates and season each with salt.

◆ Dredge fish fillets in flour, then cover in batter and then cornmeal. Fry in hot oil until golden. Drain and serve with island tartar sauce.

Serves 4

Island tartar sauce

$2/3$ cup low-fat mayonnaise

1 tbs lime juice

2 tbs chopped pineapple

salt

1 tbs chopped olives

1 tbs chopped capers

◆ Combine all the ingredients and refrigerate until ready for use.

Saltfish accras

A traditional breakfast or brunch dish, delicious with float or bakes. Also known as 'stamp and go' in Jamaica!

$1/2$ lb boneless, salted cod

juice of $1/2$ lime

2 onions, finely chopped

1 cup finely chopped chives, green and white parts

1 tsp hot pepper sauce

2 cups flour

2 tsp baking powder

oil for frying

◆ Cut salted cod into 1 inch chunks and soak overnight in cool water, changing the water about 3 times.

◆ Wash fish and flake, tasting to ensure enough salt has been removed. Drain and add lime juice.

◆ Combine fish with the onion, chives and pepper sauce. Add flour and baking powder. Pour in just enough water to make a soft and sticky batter.

◆ Heat oil in a frying pan. Drop in teaspoonfuls of batter and fry until golden on both sides.

◆ Drain and serve with floats, coconut bake or fried bakes (see pages 189, 186 and 188).

Makes 16

Jamaican ackee and saltfish

This dish is the national dish of Jamaica and has become a culinary treasure. Ackees are very tender, so you must be careful not to crush the fruit too much when cooking. When choosing ackees be sure to go for ripe ones that have turned red and are completely open, with the black seeds and yellowish fruit very visible within the reddish-colored pods. Unripe ackees do contain a toxic substance.

½ lb salted cod

10 ackees

1 tsp salt

2 pimento peppers

1 bell pepper

1 hot pepper

¼ cup olive oil

2–3 onions, sliced

2 small tomatoes, chopped

◆ Soak the cod overnight in plenty of cool water, changing the water 3 times. Drain and flake.

◆ Remove the ackees from the pods. Discard the seeds and the pink membrane found in the cleft of each fruit. Wash them and boil with the salt in a large pot of boiling water until tender, about 15 minutes. Drain and set aside.

◆ Seed and chop the peppers.

◆ Heat about 2 tablespoons oil in a frying pan, add peppers and onions and sauté for 3–4 minutes. Add the tomatoes and the fish and cook for just 2 minutes. Add the ackees and carefully turn to cook, being careful not to crush them.

◆ Remove from the heat, drizzle with the rest of the olive oil and sprinkle with freshly ground black pepper.

◆ Serve with roasted breadfruit or bakes (see page 188).

Serves 4

Shrimp and pasta rolls

1½ lb shrimp, peeled and deveined

3 tbs chopped basil

1 tsp minced garlic

salt and freshly ground black pepper

1 tbs olive oil

½ lb mushrooms, chopped

3 tbs butter

2 tbs flour

1½ cups milk

¼ tsp grated nutmeg

2 cups Italian tomato sauce

8 lasagne noodles, drained and rinsed

1 cup grated cheese

¼ cup grated Parmesan cheese

◆ Marinate shrimp in 1 tablespoon chopped basil, the garlic, salt and pepper.

◆ Heat oil in sauté pan, add shrimp and sauté just until pink and curled. Add mushrooms and toss. Remove from pan and set aside.

◆ Melt butter in a medium saucepan, add flour and cook until it becomes a smooth paste. Add milk and cook until sauce becomes thick. Season with nutmeg, salt and pepper.

◆ Remove from heat, add sauce to shrimp mixture and combine.

◆ Preheat oven to 375°F.

◆ Spread a thin layer of tomato sauce onto the bottom of a baking dish.

◆ Cut noodles in half. Place one half onto a clean surface and spoon about 1 tablespoon of shrimp mixture onto the center of the noodle. Bring both sides of the noodle over to meet in the center and place in the baking dish seam side down. Repeat for the rest of the noodles.

◆ Cover with tomato sauce, sprinkle with the remaining basil and grated cheeses.

◆ Bake until bubbly, about 20 minutes.

Serves 4

Seafood

Veggie flavors

Plantains, christophenes (also called cho-cho, chayote and tropical squash), breadfruit, eggplants, bodi (or long beans) and pumpkin are some of the more popular vegetables in the Caribbean.

Plantains, a favorite in the Spanish Caribbean, have become almost a staple in most islands. Their versatility is obvious as they are used in all stages of ripeness. A simple boiled, ripe plantain makes a healthy accompaniment to many meals. A popular way to use very ripe plantains is to slice them and fry them. Baking the sliced plantains with a sprinkling of brown sugar and nutmeg provides a delicious twist on an old favorite, as is mixing the mashed ripe plantains with herbs and grilling them. Green plantains make delicious tostones, a Spanish recipe for pounded and fried plantains. Piononos are the popular Puerto Rican dish of stuffed plantains.

Christophenes, which have a very watery consistency and flavor, are often served, especially in Grenada, in a cheesy white sauce. I've combined steamed christophenes with fresh herbs, a sprinkling of breadcrumbs and cheese to make a delightful French-style gratin. Stuffed christophenes are also very popular in the French Caribbean. Chinese vegetable stirfries often include christophenes.

Eggplant, also called melongene, is served up in many ways. I've included a stuffed version, which reflects a Syrian-Lebanese influence, and a smoked eggplant soufflé, which has a French influence.

Caribbean pumpkin, or calabaza, has a dense orange flesh, which is less watery than other types and high in flavor. In the Caribbean, pumpkin is used in many ways including as an addition to soups, stews and rice dishes.

Long beans, or bodi, as they are called in Trinidad and Tobago, are the Caribbean version of green beans. Although green beans are grown here, bodi seem to be more popular as they are very economical and very plentiful. They are included in stirfries, vegetable sautés, curries and even stews.

Breadfruit, with its starchy nature, is hard to categorize as a vegetable, or fruit for that matter. However, when in season, it is widely used across the Caribbean. It can be made into a breadfruit roll and stuffed, souffléd with fresh herbs, or served as fingers. Whichever way, it is a simply delicious and wonderful addition to any meal.

Festive scalloped potatoes

Scalloped potatoes remains one of my favorite dishes. Here is my mother's recipe, which was served to me as a child and tastes as great today as it did then.

2½ lb potatoes

5 tbs unsalted butter

5 tbs flour

4 cups milk

1½ tsp salt

1 large onion, chopped

½–1 cup grated cheese

◆ Peel and thinly slice potatoes to about ⅛ inch thickness.

◆ Preheat oven to 400°F.

◆ Melt the butter in a medium saucepan, add the flour, stirring constantly. Cook and stir until the mixture forms a creamy consistency. Add milk and stir. Lower the heat and stir until thick, smooth and creamy, about 5 minutes. Add the salt and stir. Add chopped onion, stir and remove from heat at once.

◆ Grease a casserole dish. Place a single layer of potatoes in the dish, cover with some sauce, making sure all the potatoes are covered, repeat again with another layer of potatoes and sauce. Repeat process until all the potatoes are used up, finishing with a layer of sauce. Top with grated cheese.

◆ Cover with aluminum foil and bake for 45 minutes, then remove foil and continue baking for a further 20–30 minutes until potatoes are tender and the top is lightly browned.

Serves 6–8

Spinach soufflé

Caribbean spinach tends to be the tougher variety. However, it is quite delicious when cooked.

1 tbs olive oil

1 small onion, chopped

1 tsp hot pepper, seeded and chopped (optional)

2 cups raw spinach, picked over and cleaned

¼ tsp grated nutmeg

2 tbs butter

3 tbs flour

1 cup milk

3 eggs, separated

4 tbs grated Parmesan cheese

Vegetables

◆ Heat olive oil in a large sauté pan and sauté onion until tender, about 3 minutes. Add pepper, if using, and spinach. Season with nutmeg, salt and freshly ground black pepper. Cook until spinach is wilted. Remove from heat, cool and chop finely.

◆ Melt butter in a heavy saucepan, add flour and cook until smooth. Add milk and cook, stirring, until thick. Remove from heat and whisk in egg yolks and cheese, then fold in the spinach. Taste and adjust seasoning.

◆ Preheat oven to 375°F.

◆ Beat egg whites until stiff, then fold into the spinach mixture. Spoon into a greased 9 inch soufflé dish.

◆ Bake for 30 minutes until golden and puffed.

Serves 4

Topi tambo sauté

Topi tambo is much the same as Jeruselem artichoke. Use them interchangeably.

1 lb topi tambo, boiled for 15 minutes and peeled

2 tbs vegetable oil

3 cloves garlic, chopped

juice of 2 lemons

1 tsp lemon zest

2 tbs chopped parsley

1 tbs chopped basil (optional)

◆ Slice topi tambo in half lengthways.

◆ Heat a large sauté pan and add the oil. When it is hot add the garlic and sauté until fragrant. Add topi tambo and toss. Cook for 5 minutes, then add lemon juice and lower heat. Continue to cook until the lemon juice has thickened somewhat.

◆ Season with salt and freshly ground black pepper. Sprinkle with lemon zest and fresh herbs and remove from heat.

Serves 4

Vegetables

Topi tambo and vegetable stirfry

1 tbs vegetable oil

½ tbs minced ginger

½ tbs minced garlic

1 cup cauliflower segments

1 carrot, sliced

1 large sweet pepper, seeded and cut into chunks

1 small zucchini or cucumber, sliced

½ lb topi tambo, boiled, peeled and sliced

For the sauce

1 tbs oyster sauce

1 tbs soy sauce

1 tsp sesame oil

¼ cup vegetable stock or water

½ tsp sugar

1 tsp cornstarch

◆ Mix all the ingredients for the sauce and set aside.

◆ Heat oil in wok and add ginger and garlic. Stirfry until fragrant, then add cauliflower and carrot. Stirfry for about 2 minutes, then add the pepper and zucchini with about 1 tablespoon of water to steam cook the vegetables. Add topi tambo.

◆ Add sauce and cook until bubbly and thick.

Serves 4

Stuffed breadfruit roll

This is delicious as a brunch item! Take care to work quickly with the breadfruit as it tends to become quite sticky.

2 tbs vegetable oil

1 large onion, chopped

2 tbs chopped celery

1 hot pepper, seeded and chopped

4 oz boneless, salted cod, soaked and drained

1 small breadfruit, peeled and quartered

1 tbs butter

½ cup flour

1 egg, beaten

◆ Heat the oil in a sauté pan. Add the onion, celery, pepper and salted cod and cook until flavors blend, about 10 minutes.

◆ Boil the peeled breadfruit in plenty of water until tender, about 20–30 minutes. Drain and crush. Add butter, season with salt and freshly ground black pepper and leave to cool.

◆ Add enough flour to the breadfruit to make a soft dough, and knead.

◆ Roll out breadfruit on a floured surface to make a 9 inch by 12 inch rectangle. Spread salted cod mixture onto breadfruit, keeping a 1 inch margin all the way around. Roll up breadfruit from the long side, like a jelly roll, and pinch seams together. Brush with beaten egg.

◆ Place onto a greased cookie sheet, seam side down, and bake for about 25–30 minutes until lightly browned.

◆ Cool slightly before slicing.

Serves 8

Herbed grilled plantain cakes

2 ripe plantains, peeled

¼ cup chopped chives

2 cloves garlic, minced

salt

2 tbs olive oil

◆ Boil plantains in water until tender, about 10–15 minutes. Drain and mash with a potato masher. Add the chives, garlic and salt, and stir to combine.

◆ Preheat grill.

◆ Form plantain mixture into 2 inch patties. Place on greased baking pan and brush with the olive oil.

◆ Grill until browned on each side.

Serves 4

Tostones

POUNDED 'N' FRIED PLANTAINS

These are delicious as a snack on their own but can be used as a base for appetizers with spicy shrimp or crabmeat as toppings. Always serve warm!

2 green plantains, peeled and sliced into 2 inch thick slices

vegetable oil for frying

◆ Heat oil in a frying pan and fry plantain pieces on either side until lightly browned. Remove and drain on paper towels. Cool slightly (no need to cook plantains right through at this point).

◆ With a meat pounder lightly pound plantain pieces to about ¼ inch thickness.

◆ Return pounded plantains to hot oil, and fry on both sides until golden brown. Repeat for all plantain pieces.

◆ Drain and serve warm.

Makes about 12

Souffléd breadfruit with fresh herbs

1 lb breadfruit

2 eggs, separated

2 tbs butter, melted

²/₃ cup milk

¼ cup grated Parmesan cheese

2 tbs chopped chives

2 tbs chopped parsley

1 tbs chopped thyme

½ tsp grated nutmeg

◆ Preheat oven to 375°F.

◆ Peel breadfruit and cut into 1 inch pieces.

◆ Boil breadfruit for about 15 minutes until tender. Drain and crush. With an electric mixer beat egg yolks with the melted butter and milk. Add to breadfruit, and continue beating until well combined. Add the cheese, fresh herbs and nutmeg. Season with salt and freshly ground black pepper.

◆ With clean beaters beat the egg whites until stiff. Fold into breadfruit mixture.

◆ Spoon into a greased casserole dish and bake for 30–40 minutes until golden and slightly puffed.

Serves 6–8

Vegetables

Shredded plantain fritters

1 tsp salt

1 tsp black pepper

1 tsp chili powder

2 large green plantains, peeled and grated coarsely

1 large onion, finely sliced

6 cloves garlic, minced

2 cups vegetable oil

◆ Combine the salt, pepper and chili powder.

◆ Combine the plantain, onion and garlic. Stir carefully together, the mixture will be sticky.

◆ Heat the oil in a frying pan. Using your hands or 2 spoons, form the plantain mixture into 1 inch balls, taking care not to compact the balls.

◆ Carefully drop the plantain balls into the oil. Fry until golden, about 2 minutes, turning once.

◆ Drain and sprinkle with the salt mixture.

Makes 12–15

Breadfruit fingers

2 lb breadfruit, peeled and quartered

1 tbs unsalted butter

¼ cup chopped chives

1 clove garlic, minced

salt and freshly ground black pepper

2 tbs flour

1 egg, slightly beaten

½ cup toasted breadcrumbs

vegetable oil for frying

1 tbs chopped parsley

◆ Boil breadfruit in enough salted water to cover until cooked and tender, about 20 minutes. Drain and mash with a potato masher. Add butter, chives, garlic, salt and pepper. Form mixture into fingers about 3 inches by 1 inch.

◆ Dredge fingers in flour, then dip into beaten egg and coat with the breadcrumbs.

◆ Pan fry in hot oil until golden brown on both sides. Drain on paper towels and sprinkle with chopped parsley. (Or, for a lighter dish, place fingers on a non-stick baking sheet and bake at 450°F until crusty, about 10 minutes on each side.)

Serves 4–6

Vegetables

Stuffed christophenes

Christophenes are also known as chayote. They resemble a small squash but are very watery in texture and taste.

2 medium christophenes, cut into halves, with the hearts removed

2 tbs vegetable oil

1 medium onion, chopped

2 cloves garlic, chopped

½ Congo pepper, seeded and chopped

¼ cup chopped chives

¼ tsp grated nutmeg

½ cup breadcrumbs

½ cup chopped parsley

½ cup finely grated cheese

◆ Preheat oven to 350°F.

◆ Place christophenes into a large pot of salted boiling water and cook until tender, about 20 minutes.

◆ Carefully scoop out the flesh leaving the shell intact. Mash christophenes to small chunks.

◆ Heat the oil in a sauté pan and sauté the onion, garlic, pepper and chives. Add the christophene and sauté. Add nutmeg and stir to combine. Season with salt and feshly ground black pepper.

◆ Combine breadcrumbs, parsley and cheese.

◆ Fill each christophene shell with the christophene mixture, then sprinkle with the breadcrumb mixture.

◆ Place in a shallow baking dish and bake for 20 minutes.

Serves 4

Vegetables

Stuffed christophenes

Stuffed eggplant

This dish was inspired by the famous Syrian-Lebanese version.

1 large eggplant, cut in half

3 tbs olive oil

1 onion, chopped

3 cloves garlic, minced

2 medium tomatoes, peeled, seeded and chopped

1 cup cooked rice

2 tbs chopped basil

2 tbs chopped chives

2 tbs chopped mint

1 tsp cinnamon

2 tbs grated Parmesan cheese (optional)

◆ Preheat oven to 350°F.

◆ Brush eggplant with some of the olive oil and bake in oven for about 30 minutes or until tender. Scoop the flesh out of the eggplant, leaving the skin intact.

◆ Sauté onions and garlic for 5 minutes in 1 tablespoon of the oil, add tomatoes and rice and cook for a few minutes more.

◆ Place the eggplant flesh into a food processor together with the rice mixture, basil, chives and mint. Season with salt, freshly ground black pepper and the cinnamon, and process for a couple of seconds only, to incorporate all the ingredients.

◆ Place the eggplant mixture back into the eggplant skins. Drizzle with remaining oil and sprinkle with Parmesan if wished.

◆ Bake for 30–35 minutes. Serve at once.

Serves 2–4 as a side dish

Vegetables

Christophene gratin

Here's a delightful French Caribbean dish!

1 lb tomatoes	1 tsp dried oregano	1 tsp minced garlic
3 lb christophenes	1 tsp salt	½ cup olive oil
½ cup dry breadcrumbs	1 tsp freshly ground black pepper	
½ cup chopped parsley	½ cup grated Parmesan cheese	

◆ Slice tomatoes into ¼ inch thick slices.

◆ Peel christophenes, slice in half lengthways then slice into ¼ inch thick slices. Steam christophenes with a little salt for 5 minutes, then drain.

◆ Mix together the breadcrumbs, parsley, oregano, salt, pepper, Parmesan and garlic. Add 1 tablespoon oil and combine.

◆ Lightly grease a casserole dish. Place a row of christophene, then a row of tomatoes in the dish. Continue in an overlapping fashion until all the vegetables are used up. Sprinkle with Parmesan mixture and drizzle on the remaining olive oil.

◆ Bake for 30 minutes until crust is browned.

Serves 6–8

Roasted tomatoes with fresh herbs

6 medium tomatoes, firm and ripe

1 small onion, finely chopped

¼ cup olive oil

1 cup fresh breadcrumbs

6 cloves garlic, finely chopped

1 pimento pepper, seeded and chopped

½ cup chopped parsley

1 tbs thyme

◆ Preheat oven to 400°F.

◆ Cut tomatoes in half and place in a baking dish cut side up.

◆ Sauté the onion in about 1 tablespoon olive oil until tender.

◆ Combine breadcrumbs with garlic, onion, pimento, parsley and thyme. Season with salt and freshly ground black pepper. Toss with olive oil until crumbs are moistened. Press stuffing onto tomatoes and bake until tomatoes are tender, about 30 minutes.

Serves 6

Baked plantain with brown sugar crust

Plantains are used in all their glory in the Caribbean. Be it Spanish or English Caribbean they are very popular, and not surprisingly they're very delicious too!

2 tbs brown sugar

¼ tsp grated nutmeg

4 tbs vegetable oil

2 ripe plantains, peeled and sliced lengthways into ¼ inch thick slices

1 tbs lime juice

◆ Preheat oven to 375°F.

◆ Combine the brown sugar with the nutmeg.

◆ Grease a shallow baking dish with the oil and arrange the plantain slices side by side. Brush with lime juice and sprinkle with half the sugar mixture.

◆ Bake until lightly browned, about 10–15 minutes. Turn slices over, brush with lime juice again and sprinkle with remaining brown sugar. Return to the oven and bake until the sugar is crusted and the plantain browned at the edges, about 10 minutes.

Serves 4

Vegetables

Lightly curried vegetables with garam masala

2 tbs vegetable oil

1 onion, thinly sliced

1 tbs chopped garlic

2 cumin (geera) pods

1 tbs curry powder

1/4 cup water

1 tbs chopped ginger

1 cup each potato, fresh bodi or green beans, cauliflower, carrots, cut into 1 inch pieces, you should have 4 cups

1 tsp garam masala

◆ Heat the oil in a sauté pan, add the onion and garlic and cook until lightly browned. Add cumin pods and cook until they begin to pop.

◆ Dissolve curry powder in the water and add to hot oil. Cook until thick, then add the ginger. Add potatoes and cook until tender, adding a small amount of water if needed. Add the remaining vegetables, with a small amount of water, just to prevent sticking. Cook until tender, about 5–10 minutes.

◆ Season with salt and freshly ground black pepper. Sprinkle on garam masala and serve.

Serves 4

Sautéed carailli

Carailli, better known as bitter melon, is widely used in the Caribbean in pepper sauces and pickles, stuffed East Indian style and, as in this recipe, simply sautéed and enjoyed as a vegetable side dish.

2 lb carailli, seeds removed and cut into 1/2 inch pieces

2 tbs vegetable oil

4 onions, sliced

1 tomato, chopped

2 pimento peppers, seeded and chopped

6 cloves garlic, chopped

1/2 hot pepper, seeded and chopped (optional)

◆ Salt the carailli. Leave for about 20 minutes, then squeeze and rinse under cool water.

◆ Heat the oil in a sauté pan and add onions, tomato, pimento peppers and garlic. Sauté until fragrant, then add carailli and hot pepper, if using.

◆ Cover and cook, adding only a small amount of water to prevent sticking. Cook until tender, about 15 minutes.

Serves 4

Smoked eggplant soufflé

Grilling the eggplant imparts a wonderful smoky flavor to your soufflé, but if you don't have a kitchen grill then baking or steaming will do.

3 lb eggplants

2 tbs olive oil

1 cup minced onions

4 cloves garlic, minced

1/2 cup finely chopped chives

1 tsp freshly ground black pepper

1/4 cup chopped parsley

5 tbs butter

6 tbs flour

1 1/2 cups hot milk

3 egg yolks

1/2 cup coarsely grated cheese

7 egg whites

◆ Grill, bake or steam eggplants until tender, about 20–30 minutes. Scoop out flesh and set aside.

◆ Heat the olive oil in a sauté pan and sauté onions until tender. Add garlic, chives and then the eggplant. Season with the pepper and salt to taste. Continue to cook until eggplant is tender, about 15 minutes. Add parsley, and set aside.

◆ Make the sauce by melting butter in a heavy saucepan, add flour and cook until mixture is smooth. Add milk and stir continuously until thick. Beat the yolks into the white sauce, fold in the eggplant mixture and the cheese. Season to taste.

◆ Preheat oven to 400°F. Place a roasting pan with 1 inch of water in it on a rack on the lower middle section of the oven.

◆ Beat the egg whites until stiff, then stir a quarter of them into the sauce mixture. Delicately fold in the rest of the egg whites.

◆ Turn the soufflé mixture into a baking dish. Bake for 1 1/4 hours until risen and puffed.

Serves 4–6

Vegetables

Pasta with smoked eggplant, roasted red pepper and sun-dried tomatoes

This is a great way to use eggplants, which are always in abundance on the islands.

2 sun-dried tomatoes, soaked in hot water for 15 minutes

1 large tender eggplant, about 2 lb

1 sweet red bell pepper

2 tbs extra virgin olive oil

4 cloves garlic, chopped

1 medium onion, chopped

1 lb good quality dried Italian pasta

½ cup grated Parmesan cheese

½ cup chopped basil

◆ Slice sun-dried tomatoes and set aside.

◆ Roast the eggplant over an open flame until tender and cooked. Let cool. When cool remove skin from eggplant, scoop out flesh and chop.

◆ Roast the red pepper over an open flame until blackened. Remove from heat, cover and let cool. When cooled, remove the skin and seeds and cut into strips.

◆ Heat oil in a sauté pan, add garlic and onion and sauté until fragrant. Add chopped eggplant, and stir. Add roasted red pepper and sun-dried tomatoes. Cover and continue to cook over a low heat until flavors develop, about 10–15 minutes, stirring occasionally to prevent sticking. Season with salt and freshly ground black pepper.

◆ Boil pasta in salted water according to package directions. Drain but do not rinse.

◆ Toss the vegetable mixture with the pasta and sprinkle with Parmesan cheese and basil.

Serves 6

Cauliflower with cumin and mustard seeds

2 lb cauliflower, cut into 1 inch segments

2 tbs vegetable oil

2 tsp mustard seeds

2 tsp cumin (geera) pods

1 medium onion, sliced

2 cloves garlic, chopped

2 tomatoes, diced

1/2 tsp saffron powder or turmeric

◆ Place cauliflower in a bowl and cover with water until ready for use.

◆ Heat the oil in a sauté pan and add mustard seeds and cumin pods. When they begin to sizzle and pop add the onion and garlic. Cook until onion begins to turn golden. Add tomatoes and saffron powder and cook until the tomatoes begin to soften. You may need to add a small amount of water if mixture begins to dry.

◆ Drain cauliflower and add to pan, season with salt and freshly ground black pepper.

◆ Cover and cook for 5 minutes, just until cauliflower is tender crisp.

Serves 4–6

Caribbean marinated grilled vegetables

5 cups assorted fresh vegetables, cut into 1 inch thick pieces (eggplant, bell peppers, tomatoes, onion, cauliflower, etc.)

For the marinade

1/3 cup olive oil

1 tbs fresh lime juice or red wine vinegar

3 cloves garlic

1/2 cup fresh assorted herbs (parsley, basil, chives or chadon beni)

salt and freshly ground black pepper

◆ Combine all the ingredients for the marinade and purée in a blender. Pour over the vegetable pieces and marinate for about 30 minutes.

◆ Preheat grill.

◆ Remove vegetables from marinade, thread onto metal skewers and grill for about 3 minutes per side until tender.

Serves 4

Vegetables

Piononos

STUFFED PLANTAINS

This dish originates from the Spanish Caribbean. Choose plantains that are not overly ripe, the skin should not be black. Serve with any roasted meat or poultry dish.

1 tbs vegetable oil

3 ripe plantains, peeled and sliced lengthways into 4 strips

1 tbs chopped parsley

For the filling

1 tbs olive oil

1 onion, finely chopped

2 cloves garlic, minced

1 small green pepper, seeded and finely chopped

12 oz ground beef

2 small tomatoes, skinned and finely chopped

1 tbs fresh thyme

½ cup fresh breadcrumbs

1 egg, lightly beaten

◆ Heat the vegetable oil in a large frying pan and fry the plantains until golden brown on either side, about 7 minutes. Drain on paper towels and set aside.

◆ Meanwhile, heat the olive oil, add onion, garlic and pepper, and sauté until fragrant. Add ground beef and cook until brown. Remove from heat and add the tomatoes, thyme and breadcrumbs. Fold in the beaten egg and season with salt and freshly ground black pepper. The mixture should just come together when stirred.

◆ Preheat oven to 375°F.

◆ Curve the plantain slices into rings, leaving a cavity in the centre, and secure with toothpicks. Place the plantain rings into a buttered baking dish. Fill the rings with the meat mixture and sprinkle with any unused breadcrumbs. Garnish with chopped parsley.

◆ Bake in preheated oven for about 15 minutes until the top is crusty. Serve hot.

Makes 12

Vegetables

Sautéed bodi in garlic and garam masala

Bodi or long beans are very popular in the Caribbean. They are often used interchangeably with green beans.

1 bunch bodi or 1¼ lb green beans

1 tbs vegetable oil

2 cloves garlic, chopped

½ tsp garam masala

◆ Cut bodi into 1 inch pieces and wash.

◆ Heat the oil in a non-stick skillet. Add the garlic and sauté until fragrant. Add bodi and stir and cook until bright green in color. Season with salt and freshly ground black pepper. Lower heat and cook until tender, about 10 minutes.

◆ Sprinkle on garam masala and serve.

Serves 4

Vegetables

Sautéed bodi (front) and Sautéed carailli (back, page 105)

Pumpkin vegetable stew

1 lb calabaza (crapaud) pumpkin, peeled and cut into 1 inch chunks

1 tbs vegetable oil

1 small onion, chopped

1 red bell pepper, cut into strips

1 small christophene, peeled and cubed

½ cup chopped chives

2 cloves garlic, minced

1 can (14 oz) tomatoes with juice

1 tbs chopped basil

1 tsp fresh thyme

◆ Steam pumpkin over high heat until tender. Remove and set aside.

◆ Heat oil in a sauté pan, add onion and pepper and sauté until fragrant, about 3 minutes. Add christophene and cook, covered, until tender, about 5 minutes.

◆ Add chives, garlic and tomatoes, breaking the tomatoes with the back of the spoon. Then add the basil and thyme and cook for about 10 minutes more over a low heat, covered.

◆ Season with salt and freshly ground black pepper, stir in the steamed pumpkin and turn to combine. Cook for about 1 minute more.

Serves 6

Vegetables

Rice, side and provision flavors

All through the Caribbean rice is a staple at mealtimes, and more often than not it is cooked with the addition of spices and vegetables, especially peas and beans. Pea and rice dishes have become synonymous with Caribbean food and every country has its signature dish. Cuba serves the famous black beans and rice; Jamaica's most popular rice and pea dish is red beans and rice, sometimes called 'the coat of arms'; Trinidad boasts the famous pelau, a mixture of rice, pigeon peas, beef or chicken.

Root vegetables or ground provisions owe their ancestry to the Caribs and Arawaks and abound in the islands. Every type is grown here and forms a staple at every meal. Their versatility makes them a joy to prepare and enjoy at mealtimes. Dasheen, cassava, yam, sweet potatoes and eddoe are the more popular. They can be sautéed, cooked into soups, boiled, mashed, made into cakes and fried. One of the most delicious ways to enjoy provisions is in 'oiled-down'. Also called 'run-down' in Grenada, the provisions are simmered in a seasoned coconut milk broth, too delicious to resist!

Cooked cornmeal is a popular side dish in the Caribbean. Cooked in a savory broth with ochroes and peppers, and sometimes with coconut milk, it is transformed into Caribbean polenta, or cornmeal coo-coo as it is called in Barbados and Trinidad, or fungi in the Virgin Islands. It is often served as a side to fish entrées but goes well with any saucy entrée.

Black beans and rice

Most of the islands of the Caribbean incorporate beans or peas in their rice dishes. This one is a Cuban specialty.

½ cup dried black beans

1 bay leaf

freshly ground black pepper

pinch brown sugar

1 tbs vegetable oil

2 cloves garlic, chopped

1 small onion, chopped

½ Congo or hot pepper, seeded and chopped

2 tsp ground cumin (geera)

1 cup rice

2½ cups chicken stock

¼ cup chopped chadon beni (cilantro)

◆ The night before preparing the dish soak the beans in plenty of water.

◆ Drain the beans the next morning. Place in a heavy pot, cover with water, add bay leaf, black pepper and a pinch of brown sugar. Simmer beans until tender, about 45–60 minutes. At this point make sure there is not too much water left with the beans and drain off any excess.

◆ Heat the oil in a saucepan, add the garlic, onion and pepper, and stir until fragrant. Add beans and combine, add cumin and stir. Add rice and stock. Bring to the boil, cover and simmer for about 20 minutes until cooked.

◆ Add salt to taste. Sprinkle with chadon beni.

Serves 4–6

Jamaican rice and peas

RED BEANS AND RICE COOKUP

A 'cookup' is a colloquial name given to a Caribbean dish that involves cooking several ingredients together in one pot.

1 cup dried red beans

1 bay leaf

freshly ground black pepper

pinch brown sugar

1 tbs vegetable oil

2 cloves garlic, minced

2 pimento peppers, seeded and chopped

1 Congo, habanero or scotch bonnet pepper, left whole

1 large onion, chopped

1 tbs thyme

2 cups parboiled rice

1 cup coconut milk

4 cups chicken stock

Rice . . .

◆ The night before preparing the dish soak the red beans in plenty of water.

◆ Drain the beans the next morning, place in a heavy pot, cover with water, add bay leaf, black pepper and a pinch of brown sugar. Simmer beans until tender, about 45–60 minutes. At this point make sure there is not too much water left with the beans. If there is, boil vigorously to evaporate most of the liquid. Remove bay leaf. Season the beans with salt.

◆ Heat another heavy saucepan, add the oil and heat. Add garlic, peppers, onion and

thyme. Sauté until fragrant. Add rice and toss to combine, then add the beans to pot, together with the coconut milk and stock.

◆ Bring to the boil and then lower heat and simmer for 20 minutes, covered, until rice is tender. If too wet then remove lid and let the rice dry out a bit. Remove hot pepper before serving.

Serves 4–6

Black-eyed peas and rice cookup

1 cup cooked black-eyed peas (see recipe)

1 tbs vegetable oil

1 onion, chopped

1 tbs chopped celery

1 tbs chopped thyme

2 cloves garlic, chopped

2 pimento peppers, seeded and chopped

2 tomatoes, chopped

1 cup parboiled rice

2 cups vegetable or chicken stock

½ cup coconut milk

1 tsp salt

1 hot pepper, left whole

(If you are using dried peas, soak ½ cup of black-eyed peas the night before preparing the dish, then boil with a bay leaf, a pinch of brown sugar and some black pepper for 40–60 minutes until tender. Drain.)

◆ Heat the oil in a heavy medium saucepan, and add the onion, celery, thyme, garlic and pimento peppers. Sauté until fragrant and onion is tender. Add tomatoes and cook for 1 minute longer. Add the peas and rice and turn to coat. Add stock and coconut milk, bring to the boil and season with the salt and some freshly ground black pepper. Add hot pepper and turn heat to low.

◆ Cover and steam until cooked, about 20 minutes. Remove hot pepper and serve.

Serves 4

and provisions

Dasheen salad

Dasheen is a root vegetable (provision) popular on the islands.
It is rather starchy, making it a satisfying accompaniment to any meal.

4 lb dasheen, peeled, boiled, and cut into cubes

¼ cup diced sweet red bell pepper

¼ cup diced celery

¼ cup chopped chives

¼ cup minced parsley plus chopped parsley for garnishing

4 tbs vegetable oil

3 tbs red wine vinegar

⅓ cup low-fat mayonnaise

⅓ cup low-fat sour cream or natural yogurt

1 tbs Dijon mustard

1 tsp minced garlic

salt and freshly ground black pepper

◆ Combine the dasheen with the pepper, celery, chives and parsley.

◆ In a small bowl mix the oil with the vinegar, then combine with the dasheen and set aside.

◆ Mix together the mayonnaise, sour cream, mustard, garlic, salt and pepper.

◆ Combine the mayonnaise mixture with the dasheen, and toss to coat evenly. Garnish with parsley. Refrigerate until ready for use.

Serves 10

Savory coconut rice

This is a delicious accompaniment to any hot and spicy meat or fish dish.

1 tbs vegetable oil

1 onion, chopped

1 cup parboiled rice

1 cup fresh coconut milk

1½ cups vegetable or chicken stock

1 tsp salt

1 tbs chopped chives

◆ Heat the oil in a medium saucepan, add onion and cook until tender. Add the rice and stir. Add coconut milk, stock and salt. Stir, bring to the boil, and when rice begins to make holes at the surface, reduce heat and cover.

◆ Cook until tender for about 20 minutes. Fluff with a fork, sprinkle on chives, and serve.

Serves 4

Rice . . .

Fried rice with black Chinese mushrooms and vegetables

2 tbs vegetable oil

2 eggs, lightly beaten

1 tbs minced ginger

1 tbs minced garlic

4 dried Chinese mushrooms, softened in hot water for 20 minutes, stems removed, and caps cut into ¼ inch dice

1 medium onion, finely chopped

½ cup minced chives

1 medium carrot, finely chopped

2 pimento peppers, seeded and chopped

2 tbs chopped celery

4 cups cooked rice, cooled and separated with a fork to remove lumps

For the sauce

2 tbs chicken stock or water

1½ tbs soy sauce

1 tsp salt

1 tsp sesame oil

½ tsp granulated sugar

◆ Combine the sauce ingredients and set aside.

◆ Heat a wok or large skillet, then add 1 tablespoon oil and heat until hot. Add the eggs and fry over high heat until set. Flip and remove from pot. Slice the egg.

◆ Heat remaining oil, and add the ginger and garlic. Stirfry until fragrant, add mushrooms and cook for a few minutes. Add onion, chives, carrot, peppers and celery and continue to cook until vegetables are tender, about 5–8 minutes.

◆ Return egg to pot, add rice and stirfry until heated thoroughly. Add sauce and toss to coat evenly. Serve at once.

Serves 6–8

Cornmeal coo-coo (cou-cou)

This is a Trinidadian version. The Bajan version is similar but omits the coconut milk, using only stock for liquid.

4 cups chicken stock or water

½ lb fresh ochroes, finely chopped

3 pimento peppers, seeded and chopped

2 cloves garlic, minced

salt and freshly ground black pepper

2 cups coconut milk

3 cups yellow cornmeal

◆ Boil water or stock in a large Dutch oven. Add the ochroes, peppers, garlic, salt and pepper. Simmer for 15 minutes until ochroes are tender.

◆ Add the coconut milk and return to the boil. Pour in the cornmeal, whisking vigorously to prevent lumping. Stir well and cook until the mixture becomes stiff and smooth and moves away from the sides of the pot.

◆ Generously butter a bowl. Add coo-coo to bowl and shake it around to form a ball. Leave to set. Slice and serve.

Serves 6

Caribbean pepper rice

1 tbs vegetable oil

2 cloves garlic, chopped

2 pimento peppers, seeded and chopped

1 bell pepper, seeded and chopped

1 hot pepper, seeded and chopped, or to taste

1 onion, chopped

1 carrot, grated

2 cups rice

5 cups vegetable or chicken stock

1 tbs butter (optional)

¼ cup chopped parsley

◆ Heat the oil in a medium-sized pot. Add garlic, peppers and onion, and sauté until fragrant. Add carrot and combine. Add rice and turn to coat with oil and vegetables. Then add stock and bring to the boil.

◆ Cover and simmer for about 20 minutes until rice is cooked. Season with salt and freshly ground black pepper. Add butter if using. Fluff with a fork, and sprinkle with parsley.

Serves 6–8

Rice . . .

Sweet potato soufflé

2 eggs, separated

2 tbs butter

1 small onion, chopped

2 lb sweet potatoes, boiled and crushed

1/2 cup fresh orange juice

1 tsp grated orange zest

1 tbs brown sugar

1/4 tsp grated nutmeg

◆ Beat the egg whites to soft peaks and set aside.

◆ Preheat oven to 375°F. Grease a soufflé dish or a deep casserole dish, 4 inches in depth.

◆ Heat a small sauté pan, add the butter and melt. Add the onion and sauté until tender, about 5 minutes.

◆ Place sweet potato in a mixing bowl, add onion and combine. Add egg yolks, orange juice and zest, brown sugar and nutmeg. Stir to combine. Fold in egg whites and turn into the prepared dish.

◆ Bake for 20 minutes until puffed and golden.

Serves 4–6

Sweet potato French fries

Try these French fries and I guarantee you won't eat any other! Delicious with any type of grilled meat or, of course, as an accompaniment to burgers.

2 lb sweet potatoes

vegetable oil for frying

◆ Peel and cut sweet potatoes into French fry shapes.

◆ Heat oil in a large frying pan. Dry sweet potatoes and fry in hot oil until golden and crisp, being careful not to break the fries when stirring.

◆ Drain on paper towels and serve.

Serves 4

and provisions

Cassava sauté

1 lb cassava, peeled and cut into 3 inch pieces

2 tbs vegetable oil

2 onions, sliced

2 pimento peppers, seeded and cut into strips

½ Congo pepper, seeded and chopped

2 cloves garlic, chopped

¼ cup chopped celery

¼ cup chopped parsley

2 tbs fresh thyme

◆ Place cassava into a pot, cover with water, add a pinch of salt and boil until tender, 20–25 minutes. Drain and cool.

◆ Cut cassava into 1 inch pieces, split in half, and remove center fiber.

◆ Heat the oil in a large non-stick frying pan and add onion, peppers and garlic. Sauté until fragrant, add cassava and turn and toss until the cassava pieces become coated with the onion and garlic mixture. Add celery and herbs and season with salt and freshly ground black pepper. Continue cooking over a medium heat, scraping the bottom of the pan to prevent sticking. Cook for 10 minutes, or until cassava pieces are golden in color. Taste and adjust seasonings.

Serves 4–6

Rice . . .

Cassava sauté

Herbed cassava dumplings

These dumplings are made from cassava that has been ground.
They are a great side dish with any saucy meat stew or fish dish.

1 lb cassava, peeled

1 tbs chopped parsley

1 tbs fresh thyme, chopped

2 tbs all-purpose flour

1 tsp baking powder

2 tsp brown sugar

salt

½ cup milk

olive oil for serving

◆ Place cassava into the bowl of a food processor and process until a fine paste is obtained, or grate on the fine side of a grater.

◆ Add chopped herbs to the cassava, place in a large mixing bowl and add the flour, baking powder, sugar and some salt. Adding only a little milk at a time, knead to a firm but not hard dough. Form dough into 2 inch oblong shapes, using a teaspoon to help you.

◆ Bring a large pot of water to the boil, add about ½ teaspoon of salt and when boiling drop in cassava dumplings. Cook until they float to the top of the pot, remove and serve hot, drizzled with olive oil.

Makes 16–24

Spicy Indian rice

2 cups basmati rice

¼ cup vegetable oil

1 large onion, minced

2 cloves garlic, minced

½ hot pepper, seeded and chopped

½ tsp ground cloves

½ tsp cardamom

1 tsp cinnamon

1 tsp ground cumin (geera)

¾ tsp saffron or turmeric powder

4 cups water or vegetable stock

1½ tsp salt

◆ Wash rice in plenty of cool water, then soak in water for 30 minutes. Leave to drain in colander or strainer for 20 minutes.

◆ Heat the oil in a medium saucepan. Add the onion, garlic and pepper, and sauté until fragrant. Add all the spices and turn to combine. Add rice and stir. Sauté for about 1 minute. Add the water or stock and salt.

◆ Bring to the boil and cover. Simmer until cooked for about 20 minutes.

Serves 6–8

Rice . . .

Stuffed yam cakes

Caribbean or African yams are different to the typical North American sweet or yellow yams. Caribbean yams are white, very starchy and dry, and there are no traces of sugar in them.

2 lb yams, peeled

1 tbs butter

½ cup milk

2 tbs vegetable or olive oil

1 medium onion, finely chopped

2 cloves garlic, chopped

½ Congo pepper, seeded and chopped

1 pimento pepper, seeded and chopped

1 green sweet/bell pepper, seeded and chopped

1 tbs fresh French thyme

2 tbs chopped celery

1 carrot, finely chopped

¾ cup grated cheese

¼ cup chopped parsley

◆ Cut yams into small pieces and boil in salted water for about 20 minutes or until tender. Drain yams and mash with the butter and milk. Season to taste with salt and freshly ground black pepper.

◆ Heat the oil in a saucepan and add the onion, garlic and peppers. Sauté until tender, about 5 minutes, then add thyme, celery and carrot. Cook until tender, about 10 minutes, adding a little stock or water as necessary to prevent sticking. Taste and adjust seasoning.

◆ Preheat oven to 375°F.

◆ Grease muffin or cupcake tins, and line the bases with half the mashed yams. Place the vegetable and herb mixture onto the layer of yam. Spread the remaining yam mixture onto the vegetable layer and sprinkle with grated cheese.

◆ Bake for 20 minutes until heated through. Sprinkle with chopped parsley.

Makes 12

and provisions

Vegetarian oiled-down

This is one of the most delicious Caribbean dishes I know. It is traditionally made with breadfruit, but I have found any root vegetable/provision works just as well. The root vegetables are simmered in a coconut milk broth until they become tender and creamy; each bite is infused with true coconut flavor. All the Caribbean islands have their own version of oiled-down or run-down. Here is a great meatless version which can be served on its own.

3 lb cassava

2 tbs vegetable oil

1 cup chopped onion

4 cloves garlic, chopped

1 Congo pepper, seeded and chopped, plus 1 Congo pepper left whole (optional)

2 large pimento peppers, seeded and chopped

3/4 cup chopped fresh chives, green and white parts

2 tbs chopped thyme

2 tsp salt

1 tsp freshly ground black pepper

3 cups fresh coconut milk

◆ Peel and cut cassava into 2 inch lengths. Slice the pieces down the center and remove the coarse inner vein.

◆ Heat the oil in a large heavy skillet. Add onion, garlic, chopped Congo pepper, pimentos, chives and thyme. Sauté until fragrant, about 4 minutes. Add the salt, pepper and coconut milk and bring mixture to the boil. Lower heat and add cassava. Drop in the whole Congo pepper, if using, at this point.

◆ Cover mixture and simmer for about 25–30 minutes until all the coconut milk has been absorbed and the cassava is cooked and tender. There should be only a small amount of coconut oil at the bottom of the pan when the provisions are cooked.

Serves 6–8

Vegetarian oiled-down

Curried pigeon pea pilaf

This dish is great as a main meal served with a side salad. For a lighter dish, omit the coconut milk and add another ½ cup of stock or water.

1 tbs vegetable oil

1 onion, finely chopped

2 cloves garlic, chopped

1 Congo pepper, seeded and chopped, or to taste

1 pimento pepper, seeded and chopped

1 tbs curry powder

¼ cup water

1 cup pigeon peas

1 cup parboiled rice

1 cup coconut milk

1½ cups stock or water

1 tbs chopped chadon beni (cilantro)

◆ Preheat a sauté pan or saucepan. Add the oil and heat, add onion, garlic and peppers. Sauté until fragrant.

◆ Mix curry powder with the water, add to pot, and stir until curry comes together and most of the water has evaporated. Season with salt and freshly ground black pepper. Add the pigeon peas and stir. Add the rice and toss to combine. Add coconut milk and stock or water. Stir to combine.

◆ Bring to the boil, cover and simmer for 20 minutes until rice is tender. Taste and adjust seasonings.

◆ Fluff with a fork and sprinkle with chadon beni before serving.

Serves 4–6

Yam cakes with fresh herbs

2 lb yams

1 tbs unsalted butter

¼ cup chopped chives

1 clove garlic, minced

salt and freshly ground black pepper

2 tbs flour

1 egg, slightly beaten

½ cup toasted breadcrumbs

vegetable oil for frying

1 tbs chopped parsley

Rice . . .

◆ Boil yams in salted water until cooked and tender. Drain, peel and cut into small pieces. Mash with a potato masher. Add butter, chives, garlic, salt and pepper.

◆ Form yam mixture into cakes about 2 inches in diameter. Dredge the cakes in flour, then dip into beaten egg and coat with breadcrumbs.

◆ Fry in hot oil until golden brown on both sides. Drain on paper towels and sprinkle with chopped parsley. (For a lighter dish, place yam cakes on a non-stick baking sheet and bake at 450°F until crusty, about 10 minutes on each side.)

Makes 16

Island exotic seafood paella

If you would prefer to substitute fresh vegetables for the seafood, simply add 4 cups of chunked veggies to the recipe in the same way as the seafood.

1 lb mixed seafood (shrimp, fish, squid, crab)

4 tsp minced garlic

2 tbs olive oil

salt and freshly ground black pepper

½ lime

2 cups white rice

1 large onion, minced

1 large tomato or 2 small, chopped

1 small green bell pepper, seeded and chopped

1 tsp saffron powder

4 cups vegetable stock

1 tbs fresh lemon juice

½ cup chopped parsley

◆ Clean seafood and if using fresh fish cut into 1 inch chunks. Marinate seafood in 1 teaspoon minced garlic, mixed with 1 tablespoon olive oil, salt and black pepper. Squeeze the juice from the half lime over and stir to combine. Let sit for about 10 minutes.

◆ Wash rice in several changes of water and place in a strainer until ready for use.

◆ Heat 1 tablespoon oil in a paella pan, large shallow pan, or sauté pan. Add seafood and flash fry for about 5 minutes. Remove to a bowl. Add a little extra oil to pan if needed, add onion and garlic and sauté until fragrant. Add tomatoes and green pepper, toss to combine, then add rice and turn to coat rice with the flavored ingredients in the pot.

◆ Stir saffron powder into the stock, add stock to rice in pan and bring to the boil. Cover and simmer for about 20 minutes. Return the seafood to the pot, adding all the juices from the seafood. Cover and cook for about 10 minutes more.

◆ Sprinkle with lemon juice and parsley, and serve.

Serves 4–6

and provisions

Curried vegetable and rice pelau

1 cup brown rice

1 tbs vegetable oil

2 cloves garlic, chopped

½ Congo pepper or hot pepper, seeded and chopped

1 onion, chopped

1 tsp curry powder

1 tsp ground cumin (geera)

1 tsp ground coriander

1 medium potato, peeled and cut into cubes

1 small carrot, peeled and cut into cubes

1 cup bodi or green beans, cut into 1 inch pieces

1 cup cauliflower segments

3 cups vegetable stock

1 tsp salt

¼ cup chopped chadon beni (cilantro)

◆ Wash the rice and drain.

◆ Heat the oil in a saucepan, and add the garlic, pepper and onion. Sauté until fragrant, then add curry powder, cumin and coriander and cook for a few seconds. Add the vegetables and combine to coat with the spices. Add rice and then stock. Stir to combine and add the salt.

◆ Bring to the boil then cover and simmer for 45 minutes until cooked. Sprinkle with chadon beni before serving.

Serves 4

Brown rice pilaf

1 tbs vegetable oil

1 tsp cumin seeds

1 onion, chopped

2 cloves garlic, chopped

1 tsp ground cumin (geera)

½ tsp cardamom

½ tsp turmeric

1 cup brown rice, rinsed

2½ cups chicken stock

1 tsp salt

¼ cup chopped chadon beni (cilantro)

Rice . . .

◆ Heat the oil in a heavy saucepan. Add cumin seeds and let them sizzle. Add the onion, garlic and dried spices and turn to combine. Add rice and stock and bring to the boil. Season with the salt and cover.

◆ Lower heat and cook for 45 minutes. Toss with a fork and sprinkle with chadon beni.

Serves 4

Trini Christmas festive orange rice

This rice is the perfect accompaniment to any roasted meat or poultry, especially at Christmas time! If you are using basmati rice, wash the rice in several changes of fresh water, then soak in about 4 cups cool water for 20 minutes. Drain in a colander or strainer for about 20 minutes before using.

⅓ cup almonds

2 tbs butter or margarine

1 tbs vegetable oil

1 small onion, chopped

1 tbs good quality orange marmalade

1 cup basmati or long grain rice

⅓ cup raisins

1 tsp salt

1 tsp orange zest (zest of 1 orange)

½ cup freshly squeezed orange juice

2 cups vegetable or chicken stock

2 tbs chopped celery

◆ Peel the almonds and cut into slivers. Pan fry almonds in the butter and set aside.

◆ Heat the oil in a saucepan, add onion and sauté until tender. Add the marmalade and cook until it has melted. Add the rice, raisins, salt and orange zest and stir to incorporate all ingredients. Add orange juice and stock, stir and bring to the boil.

◆ Cover and simmer until cooked, about 20 minutes.

◆ Fluff rice with a fork, turn out onto a serving platter and sprinkle with celery and almonds.

Serves 4

Chicken pelau

This is a traditional Trinidadian dish.

2 tbs minced chives

3 cloves garlic, minced

salt and freshly ground black pepper

1½ lb chicken, cut into pieces

1 tbs vegetable oil

1½ tbs sugar

2 onions, finely chopped

2 large tomatoes, chopped

2 tbs chopped celery

2 pimento peppers, chopped

¼ cup fresh French thyme

6 ochroes, sliced (optional)

1 can (14 oz) pigeon peas

2 cups parboiled rice

1 Congo pepper, left whole

1 cup coconut milk

4 cups water

◆ Combine chives with garlic, salt and pepper. Rub onto chicken and let marinate for 1 hour.

◆ Heat the oil in a large skillet. Add the sugar and leave until it has caramelized to an almost dark brown color. It will be quite bubbly and frothy.

◆ Add the chicken pieces and turn to brown evenly. Add onion, tomato, celery, pimento peppers and thyme. Combine and cook for about 5 minutes. Add the ochroes, if using, turn to combine, then add the drained pigeon peas. Add rice and turn and cook until all the ingredients in the pot are evenly coated with the seasonings.

◆ Add hot pepper, the coconut milk and water. Bring to the boil. Cover and simmer until the rice is cooked, about 20–30 minutes. Taste and adjust salt, remove hot pepper and serve.

Serves 6

Chicken pelau

and provisions

Tropical pumpkin rice

This mouthwatering rice makes an excellent accompaniment to any chicken or fish dish.

¼ lb pumpkin

2 tbs vegetable oil

1 tsp chopped garlic

2 onions, sliced

1 tbs celery, chopped

½ hot pepper, seeded and chopped

2 pimento peppers, seeded and chopped

2 cups parboiled rice

1½ tsp salt

5 cups vegetable stock

¼ cup toasted pumpkin seeds

◆ Peel pumpkin and cut into 1 inch pieces.

◆ Heat the oil in a medium saucepan, add garlic and onion, and stir until onion is fragrant. Add celery and peppers. Add the pumpkin and stir, then reduce heat and add rice. Stir to combine. Add salt and stock and bring to the boil. Cover pot and simmer for 30 minutes.

◆ Place rice in a serving dish and fluff with a fork. Garnish with pumpkin seeds.

Serves 8

Rice . . .

Cake and dessert flavors

he presence of a cake graces the table of most celebrations on the islands. The hot climate makes the survival time for cream cakes and pastries very short and as a result local cooks have perfected a butter sponge cake which is often served with or without brightly colored frostings or icing.

The most popular dessert is ice cream, found in a variety of exciting flavors, including rum and freshly made coconut. Sorbets have recently become popular, delightful flavors being passion fruit and mango.

Splendid tropical fruits used with a splash of local dark rum star in many desserts. Bananas, pineapples, papayas, limes and guavas transform most desserts into exotic masterpieces.

Mango lime pie

3½ oz ginger snaps

2 tbs melted butter

4 egg yolks

1 cup condensed milk

1 tsp lime zest

½ cup lime juice

½ cup mango purée

1 cup whipping cream (optional)

◆ Preheat oven to 325°F.

◆ In a food processor process the ginger snaps to fine crumbs. Add the melted butter and process. Press the mixture into the bottom of a 9 inch pie plate. Bake for 5 minutes until set.

◆ Increase heat to 350°F.

◆ With an electric mixer beat the yolks until light and fluffy. Add condensed milk and lime zest and mix on low speed until combined. Add the lime juice and mango purée, and mix well. Pour mixture into prebaked cookie shell and bake for 20–30 minutes until the center of the pie is firm and dry to the touch.

◆ Chill thoroughly until ready for use. Serve with whipped cream if desired.

Serves 6–8

Cakes . . .

Apple and mango streusel cake

2 apples, peeled and chopped

1 large firm half-ripe mango, peeled and chopped

For the cake

1 cup milk

1 tbs lemon juice

2 cups all-purpose flour

1 tsp baking powder

½ tsp salt

1 tsp cinnamon

½ tsp baking soda

⅓ cup unsalted butter

1 cup granulated sugar

2 eggs

2 tsp vanilla

For the topping

½ cup brown sugar

½ cup all-purpose flour

¼ cup butter

◆ Preheat oven to 350°F. Grease and flour a 9 inch baking pan.

◆ Combine milk and lemon juice and let stand until well curdled.

◆ In a large mixing bowl combine the flour, baking powder, salt, cinnamon and baking soda.

◆ Cream the butter with the sugar until light. Add the eggs one at a time, beating well between additions. Stir in the vanilla. Add the flour mixture to the creamed mixture alternately with the milk, ending with flour.

◆ Spread batter into the baking pan. Place apple and mango on top of batter.

◆ Combine the sugar and flour for the topping and rub in the butter. Sprinkle the crumb mixture over the batter.

◆ Bake for 40–45 minutes.

and desserts

Mango meringues with passion fruit cream

6 oz heavy cream

2 tsp icing sugar plus more for the finishing

2 tbs passion fruit purée

2 julie mangoes, or 2 large ripe mangoes, peeled and cut into ¼ inch cubes

2 egg whites

½ cup sugar

⅛ tsp cream of tartar

mint sprigs for garnishing

◆ Beat the cream until light, then add icing sugar and passion fruit purée. Set aside in refrigerator with the prepared mangoes.

◆ Preheat oven to 200°F.

◆ Beat the egg whites until foamy. Add the sugar gradually, followed by the cream of tartar. Continue beating until stiff and glossy.

◆ Line a baking sheet. Using a piping bag fitted with a star tube, pipe half the mixture into 3 inch circles onto the baking sheet. You should get about 4 nests. Use a knife to spread the meringue circles. Then pipe a wall around the circumference of the meringue disks.

◆ Bake meringues for 45–60 minutes until dried. Turn off oven heat and leave meringues in oven for another 30 minutes.

◆ Fill meringue nests by first adding some chopped mango, then a dollop of passion fruit cream. Finish off with more chopped mango and garnish with a sprig of fresh mint. Dust meringue nests generously with icing sugar. Chill before serving. (The meringues will keep in an airtight container for about 2 days.)

Makes 4–6

Mango meringues with passion fruit cream

Mammie apple cake

Mammie apple is a large orange-fleshed fruit found in the Caribbean. It grows on a huge tree whose timber is used in furniture-making. Its perfumed flesh makes it ideal in fruit stews and jams and jellies. You may use paw paw/papaya, fresh peaches or nectarines in this recipe.

5 large mammie apples	1 tsp cinnamon	*For the topping*
1/3 cup butter	3 tsp baking powder	1/3 cup flour
3/4 cup granulated sugar	3/4 cup milk	1 tbs butter
1 egg	1 tsp vanilla	2 tbs brown sugar
1 3/4 cups flour		

◆ Peel mammie apples by scoring the skin in sections, tearing off the skin without cutting into the fruit. Scrape off the thin brown skin which covers the fruit, ensuring all is removed. Slice the fruit off the seed and cut into uniform pieces. Set aside.

◆ Combine ingredients for the topping and set aside.

◆ Preheat oven to 350°F.

◆ Cream the butter with the sugar until light and creamy. Add egg and beat well. Sift together the flour, cinnamon and baking powder. Combine the milk with the vanilla. Add the flour and milk alternately to the creamed mixture.

◆ Pour batter into a greased and lined 9 inch springform pan or a pie plate. Arrange mammie apples on top of batter and sprinkle with topping.

◆ Bake for about 30–40 minutes, until a wooden pick inserted into the center comes out clean.

Stewed mammie apple

2 large mammie apples	1 cup water
1 cup sugar	2 tbs lemon juice

◆ Prepare mammie apples as in previous recipe.

◆ Boil sugar in water until dissolved. Add mammie apple and continue to cook on a low heat until tender, about 15–20 minutes. Add lemon juice and remove from heat.

◆ Serve as a dessert over ice cream, with yogurt, or on its own.

Serves 4

Cakes . . .

Apple mango turnovers

2 half-ripe julie mangoes, cut into small cubes

2 apples, peeled and cut into small cubes

1 tsp cinnamon

1 tbs flour

2 tbs granulated sugar

1 quantity flaky pie dough (see right)

beaten egg for brushing

◆ Preheat oven to 400°F.

◆ Combine all the ingredients except the dough in a large bowl.

◆ Roll out the dough to ¼ inch thickness. Cut into 4 inch squares using a pastry cutter or small knife.

◆ Place about 1 tablespoon of filling in the lower corner of the square, moisten the edges of the pastry with water and bring the upper piece over to cover the filling and form a triangle shape. Press with the tines of a fork to seal. Brush with beaten egg and sprinkle with granulated sugar. Place on a baking sheet. Repeat until all the pastry has been used.

◆ Bake for 10–15 minutes until light golden. Cool and remove gently from baking sheet.

Makes about 12

Flaky pie dough

2 cups all-purpose flour

1 tsp salt

8 oz shortening or 4 oz each butter and shortening

½ cup iced water

◆ Place the flour and salt in the bowl of a food processor.

◆ Cut the shortening into small pieces and drop onto the flour. Pulse in food processor until mixture resembles fine crumbs.

◆ Add the water and pulse a few times, add more water and pulse again. Continue until the mixture has curds and clumps and sticks together when pressed between your fingers.

◆ Remove and form into a ball. Wrap and chill for at least 2 hours before using.

and desserts

Coconut tarts

1 quantity flaky pie dough (see page 139)

1 quantity cooked coconut (see filling page 170)

1 egg, beaten

◆ Preheat oven to 350°F.

◆ Roll out the pastry to ¼ inch thickness and cut out 4 inch rounds. Place 1 tablespoon of filling on the bottom portion of the pastry, leaving an edge about ½ inch around filling.

Bring the top portion over the coconut to cover it, and crimp the edges with a fork to seal. Repeat until pastry and coconut are used up. Brush tarts with beaten egg.

◆ Bake for 15–20 minutes until golden. Cool on wire racks.

Makes 24

Mango cardamom sorbet

2 cups water

1 cup sugar

¼ cup fresh lime juice

¼ tsp crushed cardamom pods

2 cups mango pulp

◆ Boil water and sugar together until the sugar is dissolved. Cool, then stir in lime juice, cardamom and mango pulp.

◆ Pour into an ice cream maker and process according to manufacturer's directions.

Makes about 3 cups

Passion fruit sorbet

3 cups water

2 cups sugar

1 cup passion fruit pulp

1 tbs lime juice

◆ Make a sugar syrup by boiling water and sugar until sugar is dissolved. Leave until cold.

◆ Combine the passion fruit pulp with the lime juice and sugar syrup.

◆ Pour into an ice cream maker and process according to manufacturer's directions.

Serves 8–10

Cakes . . .

Banana sorbet

½ cup water

½ cup sugar

2 tbs lime juice

1 tbs dark rum (optional)

2 large bananas, puréed

◆ Combine water and sugar in a small pan. Bring to the boil and boil for 5 minutes until sugar is melted. Cool in refrigerator until cold.

◆ Combine syrup with lime juice and rum, if using. Whisk in the bananas.

◆ Pour into an ice cream maker and process according to manufacturer's directions.

Makes about 2 cups

Cinnamon coffee ice cream

3 tbs instant coffee

2 tbs hot water

1 cup milk

1 tsp vanilla

1 egg plus 3 egg yolks

6 tbs granulated sugar

1 tsp cinnamon

1 cup thick cream

◆ Dissolve coffee in hot water and leave to cool.

◆ Mix the milk with the vanilla. Beat the egg and yolks with the sugar until pale in color. Add the cinnamon and stir in the milk. Strain the mixture into a double boiler or pan.

◆ Heat the custard mixture slowly over a gentle heat just until the mixture thickens enough to coat the back of a wooden spoon. Do not boil or else the custard will curdle. Pour the custard into a bowl and cool.

◆ Gently stir the coffee mixture into the cooled custard.

◆ Whip the cream lightly and fold it carefully and thoroughly into the cooled custard/coffee mixture. Refrigerate until thoroughly chilled. Pour into an ice cream maker and process according to the manufacturer's directions.

Makes about 3 cups

Tropical cheesecake with ginger coconut crust
and pineapple passion fruit salsa

1²/₃ cups ginger snap crumbs

½ cup fresh grated coconut

½ cup unsalted butter, melted

For the filling

1 lb cream cheese

½ cup thick natural yogurt

³/₄ cup granulated sugar

3 eggs

2 tbs all-purpose flour

1 tsp vanilla

◆ Preheat oven to 325°F.

◆ Mix together the crumbs and coconut in a small bowl. Drizzle with melted butter; stir and toss until combined and no dry crumbs remain. Press onto bottom of an ungreased 10 inch springform pan. Bake for 5 minutes until set. Set aside.

◆ To make the filling, using an electric mixer, break up the cream cheese slightly. Add yogurt, sugar, eggs, flour and vanilla. Beat just until blended and smooth. Pour over crust and bake in preheated oven for about 1¼ hours or until center of cake is almost firm to the touch.

◆ Remove from oven and immediately run sharp knife around inside of pan. Let cool on wire rack. Chill for 4 hours or overnight.

◆ Serve with pineapple passion fruit salsa.

Serves 10–12

Pineapple passion fruit salsa

1 small ripe pineapple

½ cup passion fruit juice

½ tsp aromatic bitters

1 cup sugar

◆ Peel the pineapple, remove the eyes and chop finely.

◆ In a mixing bowl, combine the pineapple and its juices with the passion fruit juice, bitters and sugar. Stir well and check for acidity, adding more sugar if necessary.

Banana cream pie

¼ tsp salt

1¼ cups flour

½ cup shortening

¼ cup water, or more

banana slices for garnishing

For the filling

¼ cup dark rum

1 tbs gelatin

1 cup brown sugar

4 tbs cornstarch

1 cup milk

2 egg yolks

1 tsp vanilla

3 ripe bananas, puréed

1 cup whipping cream

◆ Combine the salt and flour. Add shortening and cut fat into flour until mixture resembles fine crumbs. Add water and bring dough together. Refrigerate for 1 hour.

◆ Preheat oven to 425°F.

◆ Roll out dough to fit a 9 inch pie plate. Place pastry onto plate, trim ends and crimp. Line with foil and fill with dried peas. Bake for 15 minutes. Remove foil and peas, lower heat to 350°F and continue baking for 15–20 minutes. Remove and cool.

◆ Make the filling. Gently warm the rum and sprinkle the gelatin in to dissolve. Stir.

◆ Combine sugar and cornstarch in a saucepan. Whisk in the milk and heat until mixture thickens. Beat the egg yolks. Add some of the egg to the hot custard, then add the hot custard to the remaining egg. Return to pan and heat for about 3–4 minutes.

◆ Beat in the dissolved gelatin and the vanilla. Add the banana purée. Refrigerate until cold.

◆ Whip the cream until light. Fold 1 cup into the custard.

◆ Spoon filling into tart shell, top with remaining whipped cream and garnish with banana slices.

Serves 8–10

Caribbean caramelized banana tarts

4 bananas, peeled and cut on the diagonal into 1/2 inch slices

juice of 1 lime

lime slices for garnishing

For the crust

6 tbs unsalted butter

1/4 cup granulated sugar

1 egg yolk

1 tsp vanilla

1/4 cup finely grated coconut

1 cup all-purpose flour

For the glaze

1/2 cup brown sugar

1 tbs corn syrup

1 tbs unsalted butter

◆ Prepare the crust. Cream butter with sugar until light and creamy, add the egg yolk and vanilla and stir to combine.

◆ Combine the coconut with the flour and add to the creamed mixture. Stir to make a soft dough. Cover and refrigerate until firm, about 1 hour.

◆ Heat oven to 400°F.

◆ Roll dough to 1/4 inch thickness and, using a cutter, cut out rounds about 4 inches in diameter.

◆ Bake in preheated oven for 8–12 minutes. Remove from oven and reduce heat to 375°F.

◆ Combine the banana slices with the lime juice. Arrange in a concentric circle over crust and bake for 10 minutes until bananas are tender.

◆ Make the glaze. Combine all the glaze ingredients in a heavy saucepan. Stir until bubbly and mixture begins to caramelize. Remove and drizzle over tarts. Garnish with lime slices.

◆ Serve warm with vanilla ice cream.

Makes about 6

Cakes . . .

Caribbean caramelized banana tarts

Angel food cake *with mango cardamom sauce*

This light and delicious cake is perfectly accompanied by the mango cardamom sauce, not only is it low-fat, it's enticingly exotic.

1 cup cake flour

1½ cups granulated sugar

12 egg whites

1½ tsp cream of tartar

1 tsp vanilla

whipped cream for serving (optional)

◆ Preheat oven to 375°F.

◆ Sift cake flour and combine with half the sugar.

◆ Beat the egg whites with the cream of tartar using an electric mixer until the whites are loosened. Add the vanilla. Add the balance of the sugar 1 tablespoon at a time. Beat on high speed until stiff and glossy. Be careful not to over-beat the whites or they will become somewhat lumpy in appearance.

◆ Sprinkle the flour mixture into the egg white mixture in three additions, gently folding to incorporate each addition. Again, take care not to over-mix and deflate the egg whites.

◆ Very carefully spoon batter into a 10 inch ungreased tube pan. Cut though the batter with a metal spatula to remove any air pockets.

◆ Bake for 35–45 minutes or until the cracks at the top of the cake feel dry and the top feels dry to the touch.

◆ Remove from oven, invert pan on a funnel or an empty glass bottle (a small coke bottle works well here). Leave cake inverted until completely cooled. Remove from pan and serve with mango cardamom sauce and a dollop of whipped cream if needed.

Serves 10–12

Mango cardamom sauce

2 ripe julie mangoes

1 tbs fresh lime juice

¼ tsp ground cardamom seeds

orange juice (see recipe)

◆ Peel mangoes and dice.

◆ Purée mangoes with the lime juice and cardamom. Thin with orange juice if necessary. Swirl onto plate before serving cake.

Makes 1½ cups

Cakes . . .

Stewed guava and ginger custard tart

1 cup ginger snap cookie crumbs (about 15 cookies)

2 tbs butter, melted

1½ cups milk

¼ cup sugar

1 tsp cinnamon

¼ tsp grated nutmeg

2 tbs cornstarch

2 egg yolks, lightly beaten

1 tsp vanilla

1½ cups stewed guava (see right)

¼ cup melted jam (marmalade or apricot jam)

◆ Preheat oven to 325°F.

◆ Place crumbs and butter in a mixing bowl. Toss to combine. Press this mixture into and up the sides of an 8 inch tart pan or pie plate. Bake for 3 minutes. Remove and cool.

◆ Combine the milk, sugar, cinnamon, nutmeg and cornstarch in a heavy saucepan. Stir to ensure there are no lumps. Add the egg yolks and vanilla and cook over medium heat, stirring constantly. Cook until mixture thickens.

◆ Cool and then spoon into baked crust.

◆ Arrange stewed guava on top and brush fruit with melted jam to glaze.

Serves 8

Stewed guava

12 guavas

½ cup granulated sugar

1 inch piece of cinnamon

◆ Peel guavas, scoop out seeds, and slice out the core.

◆ Place into a small pan, add the sugar and water just to come halfway up the pan. Some of the guavas will not be covered. Add cinnamon and cook slowly until fruit is tender, 15–20 minutes.

◆ Serve with custard tart or over ice cream.

Brown sugar pineapple crisp *with coconut ice cream*

1 medium pineapple

2 tsp aromatic bitters

2 tbs brown sugar

For the topping

6 tbs butter

1½ cups flour

4 tbs granulated sugar

1 tbs brown sugar

◆ Preheat oven to 350°F.

◆ Trim top and bottom from pineapple, peel and remove eyes. Cut pineapple in half lengthways, then into quarters. Remove inner core and cut into 1 inch chunks.

◆ Combine bitters with pineapple and brown sugar, and place into a greased casserole dish.

◆ Make topping by combining the butter with the flour until the mixture resembles fine crumbs. Add the granulated sugar. Clump the mixture together with your hands, and cover the pineapple with this mixture, making sure that all the fruit is covered. Sprinkle with brown sugar.

◆ Bake for about 35–40 minutes until crisp and bubbly. Serve with coconut ice cream.

Serves 6

Coconut ice cream

4 egg yolks

½ cup granulated sugar

1 cup milk

2 cups fresh coconut milk

⅔ cup condensed milk

2 tsp vanilla

6 oz heavy cream

◆ Make a custard by whisking the egg yolks with the sugar. Add milk and cook in a double boiler, stirring, until mixture is thick and coats the back of a wooden spoon. Remove and stir in the coconut milk, condensed milk, vanilla and cream. Refrigerate until cold.

◆ Pour mixture into a ice cream maker and process according to manufacturer's directions.

Makes about 1 litre

Cakes . . .

Coconut ice cream

Pineapple cheesecake pie

For the crust

2 cups ginger snap cookie crumbs

4 tbs sugar

1/3 cup butter, melted

For the filling

2 tbs gelatin

2 tbs warm water

1/2 cup pineapple juice

3 eggs, separated

3/4 cup granulated sugar

1 lb cream cheese

1 cup crushed pineapple, drained (fresh or canned)

2 cups whipped cream

pineapple and mint leaves for garnishing

◆ Preheat oven to 325°F.

◆ Combine crust ingredients and press into the bottom of a 10 inch pie plate. Bake for 5 minutes until just firm. Leave to cool.

◆ Dissolve gelatin in the warm water, and gently warm until melted. Add pineapple juice and combine. Beat egg yolks with 1/2 cup sugar, add to gelatin mixture and cook over low heat until thick, about 5 minutes. Remove and cool.

◆ Beat egg whites, with clean beaters, until frothy. Add the remaining sugar and continue beating until stiff peaks form.

◆ Beat cream cheese until smooth, add egg and gelatin mixture and fold in the crushed pineapple and combine. Fold in whipped cream and egg whites. Spoon into prepared crust and chill overnight until firm.

◆ Garnish with pineapple and mint.

Serves 8–10

Cakes . . .

Free-form mango almond tart

You can use apples or pears instead of mangoes in this recipe.

3 medium mangoes, preferably julie, half-ripe

1 tbs fresh lime juice

2 tbs finely chopped almonds

½ cup granulated sugar

2 tbs all-purpose flour

For the pastry

1½ cups all-purpose flour

1 tbs granulated sugar

pinch salt

¾ cup unsalted butter

¼ cup iced water

◆ Make the pastry. Combine the flour with the sugar and salt in a large bowl. Rub butter into flour until the mixture resembles fine crumbs. Sprinkle water over the mixture. Bring pastry together lightly with your hands and chill for 15 minutes before rolling out.

◆ Peel mangoes and slice off the seed. Chop coarsely. Sprinkle with lime juice.

◆ Preheat oven to 400°F.

◆ Roll pastry into a rectangle approximately 16 inches by 2 inches. Place on a cookie sheet.

◆ Combine the nuts, half the sugar and the flour. Sprinkle over pastry to within 1 inch of border. Place mangoes over nuts, then fold pastry to partly cover the mango, bringing it about 2 inches over the fruit. Sprinkle with remaining sugar.

◆ Bake for 35–40 minutes until fruit is tender and pastry is browned.

Serves 8

Grilled pineapple

1 small pineapple, peeled and cut into spheres

2 tsp aromatic bitters

¼ cup brown sugar

◆ Place the pineapple in foil and sprinkle with the bitters and sugar. Wrap and place on grill. Grill for about 15 minutes until tender and sugar has begun to caramelize. At this point you may remove it from foil and finish directly on the grill.

◆ Serve with ice cream.

and desserts

Orange caramel flan

1⅓ cups sugar

4 eggs

1½ cups milk

¼ tsp grated nutmeg

1 tsp vanilla

1 tsp grated orange zest

◆ Preheat oven to 350°F.

◆ In a heavy-bottomed saucepan, melt 1 cup sugar to a caramel color. Do not burn, your caramel is ready when you begin to smell the caramel.

◆ Pour caramel into the bottom of a glass pie plate, swirling the plate to cover the base. Set aside.

◆ Beat the eggs in a bowl with the remaining sugar and milk. Add nutmeg, vanilla and orange zest. Strain mixture and pour into caramel-lined plate.

◆ Place pie plate into a pan of water and bake for 50–60 minutes until a knife inserted into the center comes out clean.

◆ Remove and cool. Invert before serving.

Serves 4–6

Bananas flambé *with rum-infused ice cream*

3 tbs unsalted butter

½ cup brown sugar

1 tsp cinnamon

4 ripe bananas, peeled and cut into quarters lengthways

½ cup dark rum

1 splash aromatic bitters

◆ Melt the butter in a heavy skillet over moderate heat and add the brown sugar and cinnamon. Stir until mixture begins to bubble. Add the bananas and sauté for a few minutes on each side.

◆ Add the rum and bitters and ignite with a match. Let it burn briefly and then smother the flame with a heavy pot cover.

◆ Continue to cook for a further 3 minutes. Serve with rum-infused ice cream.

Serves 4

Cakes . . .

Rum-infused ice cream

4 egg yolks

1/2 cup granulated sugar

2 cups full cream or evaporated milk

2 cups whipping cream

1/4 tsp grated nutmeg

2 tbs grated orange zest

1/4 cup rum

◆ Beat the egg yolks with the sugar until light. Add milk and cook, stirring, over low heat until thick. Be careful not to boil. Cool mixture.

◆ Lightly whip cream and fold into chilled custard mixure. Add nutmeg and orange zest. Stir in rum.

◆ Chill mixture and place in ice cream maker. Process according to manufacturer's instructions.

Makes 1.5 litres

Decadent chocolate ripple cheesecake

20 chocolate cookies

4 tbs melted butter

4 oz semi-sweet or bitter sweet chocolate

1 lb cream cheese

1/2 cup granulated sugar

3 eggs

1 tsp vanilla

1/2 cup natural yogurt

◆ Preheat oven to 350°F.

◆ Finely crush cookies in a food processor. Add melted butter and combine. Press mixture into the bottom of a 9 inch springform pan and refrigerate.

◆ Break the chocolate into small pieces and place in a small saucepan. Place the saucepan into a larger pan (a skillet works well here), half filled with simmering water. Gently stir chocolate until it melts, taking care not to burn it. Set aside.

◆ With an electric mixer, beat the cream cheese until creamy. Add sugar, eggs and vanilla and beat until smooth. Gently beat in the yogurt.

◆ Drizzle melted chocolate into cream cheese mixture and fold just until incorporated. Do not stir or fold too vigorously or you will not get the ripple effect.

◆ Pour batter into cookie crust and bake for 40–50 minutes until cheesecake is slightly puffed and the centre is set.

◆ Refrigerate for 4 hours or overnight.

Serves 8–10

> You can wrap the springform pan in foil during baking to prevent any liquid from dripping through the seam of the pan.

and desserts

Fruited cheesecake trifle

½ cup granulated sugar

4 egg yolks

2 tsp vanilla

1 lb cream cheese, cut into pieces

1½ cups whipping cream

¼ cup dark rum (optional)

1 can (28 oz) peaches, drained, reserving juice, and chopped

20 Italian lady finger biscuits or one 12 oz butterless sponge cake cut into 3 inch by 1 inch pieces

½ cup toasted almonds

glacé cherries for garnishing

◆ With an electric mixer beat the sugar with the egg yolks until thick and fluffy. Add vanilla and continue beating. Add cream cheese and beat until smooth. Refrigerate for about 1 hour or until chilled.

◆ Beat the whipping cream until stiff and fold into the cream cheese mixture. Cover and refrigerate until ready to use.

◆ Add rum, if using, to ½ cup reserved peach juice. Otherwise, use ¾ cup peach juice.

◆ Line the base of a glass dish with sponge pieces and sprinkle with juice mixture or dip lady fingers into juice and arrange at the bottom of your dish. Top with half the peaches and half the cheese mixture. Repeat with another layer of lady fingers, peaches and cream cheese mixture.

◆ Sprinkle on the toasted almonds, garnish with cherries and cover with plastic wrap. Refrigerate for 4 hours or overnight.

Serves 8–10

Cakes ...

Pineapple upside-down cake *with passion fruit cream*

$\frac{1}{3}$ cup unsalted butter plus 2 tbs	$\frac{3}{4}$ cup milk
$\frac{3}{4}$ cup granulated sugar	1 tsp vanilla
1 egg	$\frac{1}{4}$ cup brown sugar
$1\frac{3}{4}$ cups all-purpose flour	1 can (14 oz) pineapple rings, drained (about 9)
3 tsp baking powder	9 maraschino cherries

◆ Preheat oven to 350°F.

◆ Cream $\frac{1}{3}$ cup butter with the granulated sugar until light and fluffy. Add the egg and beat well. Sift the flour with the baking powder then add to butter mixture alternately with milk and vanilla, making sure your last addition is with flour.

◆ Melt 2 tablespoons butter in a 9 inch cake pan. Add the brown sugar and stir to melt. Do not brown. Remove from heat. Arrange pineapple rings onto cake pan. Place a cherry in each ring. Pour on cake batter and bake for 35 minutes.

◆ Remove, and invert onto serving plate. Serve with passion fruit cream.

Serves 8

Passion fruit cream

1 cup whipping cream

1 tbs passion fruit purée

2 tbs powdered sugar

◆ Beat cream until light and stiff. Add sugar and passion fruit purée, stir, and refrigerate until ready for use.

and desserts

Rummy pineapple shortcakes with cream

For the shortcakes

2 cups cake flour

4 tbs brown sugar

1 tbs baking powder

½ tsp baking soda

1 tsp cinnamon

¼ tsp grated nutmeg

¼ cup butter

¼ cup vegetable shortening

1–1½ cups sour cream or yogurt

2 tbs milk

For the custard

3 egg yolks

¼ cup granulated sugar

½ tsp cinnamon

2 tbs cornstarch

1 tsp vanilla

1 cup milk

For the pineapple topping

⅓ cup unsalted butter

½ cup brown sugar

1 small pineapple, peeled, cored and finely chopped

1 tsp aromatic bitters

¼ cup dark rum (optional)

◆ Preheat oven to 400°F.

◆ Combine dry shortcake ingredients. Rub butter and shortening into mixture until it resembles fine crumbs. Add enough sour cream or yogurt to make a soft manageable dough.

◆ Pat or roll dough into a circle about 1½ inches thick. Cut out rounds 2½ inches in diameter or cut into 2½–3 inch squares. Brush with milk.

◆ Place on a greased cookie sheet and bake for 15 minutes until golden. Remove and cool.

◆ Make the custard. Beat the eggs with the sugar until thick. Add cinnamon and cornstarch and continue beating. Add the vanilla.

◆ Heat milk, pour into egg mixture and beat. Return to pan and heat until mixture thickens, do not boil. Strain and cool.

◆ To make topping, heat a non-stick frying pan, add butter and melt. Add brown sugar and combine with butter until melted, but not burnt. Add pineapple and sauté, then add bitters and cook until mixture is thick. Pour on rum, if using, and flambé. Let flames burn down and continue to cook until syrupy.

◆ To assemble, halve one shortcake horizontally, spoon pineapple mixture onto one piece, cut side up, making sure some of the juices soak into the cake. Spoon some custard on top and cover with the other shortcake half. Repeat for other shortcakes. (For a more hearty dessert sandwich two shortcakes together instead of splitting one.)

Makes 8

Tropical bread pudding *with rum sauce*

1 cup boiling water

⅓ cup raisins

1 tsp aromatic bitters

3 cups milk

4 eggs

½ cup granulated sugar

2 tsp vanilla

½ tsp grated nutmeg

1 tsp cinnamon

1 loaf good quality white or egg bread

◆ Preheat oven to 350°F. Butter an 8 inch baking dish.

◆ Pour the boiling water over raisins, add bitters, and allow to soak for 10 minutes.

◆ Heat milk in saucepan.

◆ Beat the eggs with the sugar in a mixing bowl. Add warm milk, vanilla, nutmeg and cinnamon.

◆ Cut bread into 1 inch cubes, pour custard over bread cubes, and add raisins. Pour mixture into prepared dish.

◆ Bake in a water bath for about 50–60 minutes.

◆ Cool pudding a little and serve warm, with rum sauce.

Serves 8

Rum sauce

1 cup brown sugar

1 cup evaporated milk or light cream

¼ cup dark rum

◆ Melt the sugar in a heavy saucepan and cook until it turns a caramel color. Averting your face, add the milk gently. It will bubble vigorously. Stir until smooth. Strain.

◆ Add rum and serve warm.

Makes about 1½ cups

Cheesecake with ginger crust

2 cups ginger snap cookie crumbs

4 tbs sugar

⅓ cup butter, melted

almonds for garnishing (optional)

For the filling

1 lb cream cheese

¾ cup sugar

3 eggs

½ cup low-fat yogurt

◆ Preheat oven to 325°F.

◆ To make the crust, combine the crumbs with the sugar and add the melted butter. Press into the bottom of an 8 inch springform pan. Bake for 5 minutes until set. Set aside.

◆ Increase heat to 400°F.

◆ With an electric mixer combine cream cheese and sugar, then add the eggs one at a time until well mixed and mixture is smooth. Fold in yogurt. Pour over crust and bake for 10 minutes.

◆ Lower temperature to 250°F and continue to bake for another 60 minutes.

◆ Remove cake from oven and run a knife gently around the rim of the pan to loosen the cake. Cool completely on a wire rack before removing from the pan.

◆ Garnish with almonds, if desired, and serve with fresh fruit.

Serves 10–12

Cakes . . .

Bajan conkies

These are spiced and steamed cornmeal coconut puddings. They are wrapped in banana leaves before steaming (but if you don't have banana leaves you can wrap the conkies in aluminum foil). Bajans love these delights, and it is rumored that when someone is making conkies there's always a line of conkie lovers outside his/her door! They are traditionally served on Independence Day in Barbados – November 30.

2 cups grated fresh coconut

³⁄₄ lb pumpkin, peeled and grated

¹⁄₂ lb sweet potato, grated

¹⁄₂ cup flour

2 cups brown sugar

2 cups cornmeal

4 oz raisins or other dried fruit

1 tsp cinnamon

1 tsp grated nutmeg

¹⁄₂ cup butter, melted

1 cup water

1 tsp vanilla

8 banana leaves, 8 inches square

◆ In a large mixing bowl combine coconut, pumpkin, sweet potato, flour, sugar, cornmeal, dried fruit and dried spices.

◆ Combine butter with water and pour into dry mixture. Add vanilla and stir to mix. The mixture should be of the consistency of wet dough. If it seems too dry then add a little more water.

◆ Prepare banana leaves by steaming for 10 minutes to soften.

◆ Put 2 tablespoons of mixture onto the center of each leaf and fold into a neat rectangular package. Tie with string.

◆ Steam for about 45–60 minutes. Serve warm or cold.

Makes 8

and desserts

Caribbean crepes with roasted pineapple salsa and passion fruit butter

½ cup all-purpose flour or cake flour

pinch grated nutmeg

1 tbs sugar

¼ cup milk

¼ cup water

1 egg and 1 egg yolk

1 tbs melted butter

1 tbs rum plus ¼ cup

For the salsa

1 medium fresh pineapple, peeled and cut into segments

2 tsp aromatic bitters

⅓ cup brown sugar

For the butter

¼ cup orange juice

2 tbs passion fruit purée

¼ cup sugar

1 oz unsalted butter

Cakes . . .

- Make the salsa. Combine all the ingredients. Place under the broiler for about 5–8 minutes until lightly browned and sugar has melted and caramelized. Cool and chop finely.

- Place flour, nutmeg and sugar in a mixing bowl. Whisk in milk and water until smooth, then add eggs and continue whisking. Add melted butter and 1 tablespoon rum and combine. Cover and rest for 1 hour in the refrigerator.

- Heat a non-stick frying pan, about 5 inches in diameter, and pour in about ¼ cup of crepe batter. Tilt pan until batter is almost transparent (if the batter seems too much in the pan, pour off excess). Flip over when bubbles appear, cook for a few seconds more and remove. Repeat until all the batter is used.

- Combine all ingredients for the fruit butter in a food processor. Place in a large frying pan and cook until thick and bubbly. Add crepes to pan and bathe in fruit butter. Fill with salsa, fold into quarters, pour on remaining rum and flambé. Serve warm. (If the pan is not large enough to accommodate all the crepes, prepare in batches, reserving some fruit butter for each batch.)

Makes 8

Light Christmas fruit cake with cherries and walnuts

1 cup unsalted butter

1 cup granulated sugar

4 eggs

½ cup glacé cherries, finely chopped

½ cup raisins

½ cup mixed peel

½ cup chopped walnuts

2 cups all-purpose flour

- Preheat oven to 325°F. Grease, line and flour a 9 inch round cake pan.

- With an electric mixer, cream butter and sugar until light and creamy, about 5 minutes.

Add eggs one at a time, beating well between additions.

- Combine cherries, raisins, mixed peel and walnuts.

- Sift flour. Remove 2 tablespoons of flour and combine this with the fruit and nut mixture. Toss to coat evenly.

- Gently fold flour and fruits into batter. Pour batter into the prepared pan.

- Bake for about 1½ hours. Cool.

Best ever Christmas cake

1 lb raisins	1²/₃ cups cherry brandy	1 tsp cinnamon and allspice, mixed
½ lb currants	1 lb butter	¼ lb glacé cherries plus extra for decorating (optional)
½ lb sultanas	1 lb brown sugar	½ lb chopped walnuts
½ lb prunes	6 eggs	2 tsp mixed essence
¼ lb mixed peel	1 lb all-purpose flour	
1²/₃ cups dark rum	3 tsp baking powder	

◆ Seed and cut up fruits, except cherries, into ¼ inch pieces.

◆ Combine the rum and cherry brandy and add fruits to mixture. Let soak overnight or up to 1 week.

◆ Preheat oven to 300°F.

◆ Cream butter and sugar until light and fluffy. Add eggs one at a time, beating well after each addition.

◆ Sift together the flour and baking powder, cinnamon and allspice.

◆ Drain the fruits, reserving the liquid. Add drained fruits to creamed mixture.

◆ Roughly cut up the cherries and nuts and add to the mixture, then fold in the flour. Add mixed essence and mix well.

◆ Grease and line two 9 inch cake pans with waxed paper. Grease and flour the paper.

◆ Spoon the cake batter equally into the prepared baking pans. Bake for 2–2½ hours.

◆ Pour reserved rum and cherry brandy mixture over cake when baked. Cool in pans before removing. Decorate with extra cherries if wished.

Makes 2

Best ever Christmas cake

and desserts

The best butter sponge cake

Caribbean people love to eat cake and this butter sponge is the all-round favorite!

3 cups cake flour

1 tbs baking powder

½ tsp salt

8 oz butter

2 cups granulated sugar

4 large eggs

1 tsp vanilla

1 cup milk

◆ Preheat oven to 350°F. Grease and flour two 9 inch cake pans.

◆ Sift the flour three times and add the baking powder and salt. Set aside.

◆ With an electric mixer, cream the butter with the sugar until light and creamy, about 10 minutes. Add the eggs one at a time, beating well between additions. Add the vanilla. Reduce the mixer speed to medium low or low. Add the flour to the mixture alternately with the milk, in four additions, starting and ending with the flour. Mix until just incorporated after each addition.

◆ Divide the batter evenly between the pans. Bake for 35–40 minutes, or until the cake pulls away from the side of the pan.

◆ Remove from oven and cool for 5 minutes in pans before turning out. Sandwich with chosen filling.

West Indian chocolate cake

Cocoa is commonly used in the West Indies. However, the results are just as superb as with real chocolate.

1 cup butter	4 tsp baking powder	4 eggs
2 cups granulated sugar	1 tsp baking soda	2 tsp vanilla
2¼ cups all-purpose flour	1 cup cocoa powder	1 cup milk

Cakes . . .

◆ Preheat oven to 350°F. Grease sides and bases of two 9 inch cake tins and line with waxed paper.

◆ Cream butter and sugar until light and fluffy and doubled in volume.

◆ Sift flour three times, add baking powder and baking soda. Sift cocoa and combine with flour.

◆ Add eggs one at a time to creamed mixture, making sure to beat well between additions. Batter must be fluffy.

◆ Add vanilla to milk. Add flour to batter alternately with milk in four additions, beginning and ending with the flour mixture. Spoon batter evenly into prepared tins.

◆ Bake for 35–40 minutes until done and cake pulls away from the sides of the tin.

Makes 2

Fluffy boiled frosting

3 egg whites

⅛ tsp cream of tartar

2 cups granulated sugar

⅓ cup water

◆ Using an electric mixer beat the egg whites until fluffy but not dry. Add the cream of tartar.

◆ Combine the sugar with the water in a small saucepan. Stir gently and bring to the boil. Boil sugar until it is bubbly and spins a thread when lifted from a fork.

◆ Pour syrup into egg whites with mixer running. Continue to beat until all the syrup has been incorporated. Beat for a few minutes longer until mixture loses some of its gloss.

Frosts two 9 inch cakes

Chocolate butter frosting

4 cups icing sugar

½ cup cocoa powder

½ cup butter

2 tbs evaporated milk

◆ Sift icing sugar with cocoa powder and combine. Cream butter and gradually add icing sugar and cocoa mixture. Add a couple of drops of milk at a time to bring the frosting to a creamy consistency.

Frosts two 9 inch cakes

and desserts

Cocoa coffee cake

Cocoa is grown in the Caribbean and locally processed in Jamaica, where some of the better cocoa is available. Cocoa powder is traditionally used a lot in Caribbean baking, while block chocolate is seldom used.

½ cup unsalted butter

¾ cup granulated sugar

2 eggs

2 tsp baking powder

1½ cups flour

⅔ cup milk

⅓ cup cocoa

⅓ cup chopped walnuts

⅓ cup brown sugar

1 tsp cinnamon

icing sugar to finish

◆ Preheat oven to 350°F. Grease a 9 inch cake pan.

◆ Cream butter with granulated sugar until creamy. Add the eggs and beat until nice and fluffy. Combine the baking powder and flour and add to mixture alternately with the milk.

◆ Combine cocoa, nuts, brown sugar and cinnamon. Place a third of the batter into pan, sprinkle with half the cocoa mixture. Repeat with another layer of batter, then cocoa mixture. Top with remaining batter.

◆ Bake for 30–35 minutes. Remove from oven. Cool and sprinkle with icing sugar.

Cakes . . .

Bread and sweet bread flavors

Bakeries are quite abundant in the Caribbean islands, and a visit to any would reveal a variety of breads and sweet breads. But true Caribbean breads can mostly be found in the home where they are baked just before serving at mealtimes. The most popular are rotis and bakes.

Rotis are an East Indian legacy found mostly in Trinidad and Tobago and Guyana, but their popularity has spread to other Caribbean islands and worldwide. These are really flatbreads, served with curries or cooked vegetables. There are a variety, the most popular being dhalpourie, which is filled with seasoned split peas and baked on a baking stone. This type of filled roti can be found in any roti shop on the islands. Roti shops are popular fast food outlets. Then there is paratha roti, a flaky roti with butter rolled into the dough. The roti is then torn apart after cooking giving a broken-up effect, hence the more familiar name 'buss up shirt'. Sada roti, which resembles a thick flour tortilla, is cooked, split into half and often filled with cooked vegetables.

Bakes are the Creole legacy. They can either be fried or baked, leavened with yeast or baking powder, either way they are quick and simple to make. The most popular bake is coconut bake, made with the addition of fresh coconut milk and grated coconut. Bakes are usually enjoyed with fish buljols or fried fish at brunch or breakfast time.

Every bakery in the Caribbean has its version of what is fondly called sweet bread. These breads are delicious local breads made with flour, dried fruit, grated coconut, flavorings and ground spices. Some of them may be lighter in texture than others. Sometimes they are made into small buns and sugared at the top and other times they are made in loaf pans.

Coconut is used in many ways, one of the more delicious being cooked with sugar and spices, rolled into a dough and baked.

Big banana bran bread

½ cup butter

1 cup brown sugar

2 eggs

1 cup mashed ripe bananas (about 3–4 bananas)

1 tsp lime zest

½ cup milk mixed with ½ tbs lime juice

1 tsp vanilla

1 cup bran flakes

2 cups all-purpose flour

1 tbs baking powder

½ tsp baking soda

½ tsp salt

2 tsp cinnamon

½ tsp grated nutmeg

¼ tsp allspice

½ cup chopped walnuts (optional)

◆ Preheat oven to 350°F.

◆ In a large mixing bowl, with an electric mixer, cream butter and sugar until light. Add eggs and beat until fluffy. Add bananas, lime zest, milk and vanilla.

◆ Combine all the dry ingredients in a medium-sized bowl. Add the dry mixture to the banana mixture and stir just until moistened. Fold in the nuts, if using.

◆ Pour into a greased 9 inch by 5 inch loaf pan.

◆ Bake for 50–55 minutes until a wooden pick inserted into the center comes out clean. Remove from pan and cool completely before slicing.

Light coconut sweet bread

Each island has its own version of coconut breads, sweet breads or spiced breads. Here is my favorite, not too heavy and not too sweet. This is a great breakfast or tea time bread and it makes great toast.

½ cup raisins

4½ cups all-purpose flour

½ cup freshly grated coconut

1 tbs cinnamon

1 packet instant yeast

1 cup coconut milk

⅓ cup butter, melted

⅓ cup sugar

½ tsp salt

2 eggs

sugar syrup (see glaze, page 170)

¼ cup brown sugar

◆ Soak raisins in warm water.

◆ In a mixer bowl combine 2 cups flour, the coconut, cinnamon and yeast. Heat the coconut milk, butter, sugar and salt to 115°–120°F. Add to flour mixture.

◆ Add eggs and beat slowly until incorporated. Add drained raisins and incorporate. Add as much of the remaining flour as you can, then turn onto a floured surface and knead to make a moderately stiff dough that is smooth and elastic, about 6–8 minutes.

◆ Place in a greased bowl, cover and let rise until doubled in bulk, about 45 minutes.

◆ Punch down, divide in half and rest dough for 10 minutes.

◆ Shape into loaves and let rise for another 45 minutes until doubled in size.

◆ Preheat oven to 350°F. Bake for about 30 minutes until brown. Glaze with sugar syrup and sprinkle with brown sugar.

Makes 2 loaves

Orange-perfumed coconut roll

Cooked coconut is juicy, flavorful and delicious. When choosing coconuts, shake your coconut – you should hear a slight sloshing sound from a small amount of liquid inside. This is a good indication that your coconut is fresh!

1 cup milk

4–4½ cups all-purpose flour

1 tbs instant yeast

2 tsp grated orange zest

1 tsp salt

2 tsp cinnamon

⅓ cup brown sugar

2 eggs

2 tbs melted butter

For the filling

2 cups freshly grated coconut

2 cups granulated sugar

4 cloves, ground

2 tsp cinnamon

For the glaze

¾ cup sugar

½ cup water

◆ Warm milk to 115°–120°F.

◆ Combine 2 cups flour with the yeast, orange zest, salt, cinnamon and sugar. Add milk to the flour mixture and beat in the eggs with an electric mixer. Add enough flour to make a sticky dough.

◆ Turn onto a floured surface, and knead in enough flour to make a smooth elastic dough. Place in a mixing bowl, cover and let rise until doubled in volume.

◆ Make the filling. Place the coconut and sugar in a medium saucepan. Cook on medium heat until mixture begins to bubble. The mixture should water a little. Add spices and continue cooking, stirring frequently, until mixture comes together, about 20 minutes. You can add a small amount of water if needed to prevent sticking. Remove coconut when it is cooked and still juicy, do not dry your mixture out. Leave to cool.

◆ Make the glaze. Cook sugar in the water until melted and syrupy. Remove and cool.

◆ Divide dough in half and roll each piece into a 12 inch by 8 inch rectangle. Spread with melted butter. Then spread each half with half of the coconut mixture, leaving a 1 inch margin around each piece of rolled dough.

◆ Roll up each piece jellyroll style, beginning from the longest end. Pinch edges of dough together to seal and place seam side down onto lined baking sheets. Cover and let rise until doubled in size, about 15–20 minutes.

◆ Preheat oven to 375°F.

◆ Bake for 20–25 minutes until golden. Glaze with sugar syrup and sprinkle with brown sugar, then bake for 5 minutes longer. Cool before slicing on the diagonal.

Makes 2

Orange-perfumed coconut roll

Pineapple upside-down muffins

3 tbs butter

½ cup brown sugar

1 cup fresh or canned pineapple chunks, drained

½ tsp aromatic bitters

12 maraschino cherry halves

2 cups all-purpose flour

¼ cup granulated sugar

1 tbs baking powder

½ tsp cinnamon

2 eggs, beaten

½ cup milk

⅓ cup vegetable oil

1 tsp vanilla

◆ Preheat oven to 375°F.

◆ Melt the butter in a sauté pan or non-stick frying pan, and add brown sugar. Cook just until sugar bubbles, do not darken or burn. Add pineapple and bitters and toss to coat well. Remove from heat.

◆ Spoon pineapple into 12 muffin cups, arranging in a pattern. Place a cherry half into each cup. Set aside.

◆ In a mixing bowl combine the flour, sugar, baking powder and cinnamon. Beat the eggs with the milk and oil, then add the vanilla. Add the wet ingredients all at once to the dry and stir just until combined.

◆ Spoon into prepared muffin tins and bake for 18–20 minutes. Invert muffins onto a wire rack to cool.

Makes 12

Spiced hot cross buns

These are eaten on Good Friday morning, but I can have them anytime!

1 tbs active dry yeast

¼ cup warm water

1 cup lukewarm milk

⅓ cup brown sugar

⅓ cup butter, melted

1 tsp salt

2 tsp cinnamon

¼ tsp ground cloves

¼ tsp grated nutmeg

1 egg and 1 egg yolk

4–4½ cups all-purpose flour

1 cup raisins

½ cup mixed citron peel

1 egg white, slightly beaten

◆ In a large bowl, dissolve the yeast in the water and stir in the milk, sugar, butter, salt, cinnamon, cloves, nutmeg, egg, egg yolk and 2 cups flour. Beat until smooth. Stir in raisins and mixed peel and add enough flour to make the dough easy to handle.

◆ Turn dough onto a lightly floured surface and knead until smooth and elastic, about 5 minutes. Place in a greased bowl and turn the greased side up. Cover and let rise until doubled in bulk, about 1½ hours.

◆ Punch down dough and divide into 4 equal parts. Cut each part into 6 equal pieces and shape each piece into a ball. Place about 2 inches apart on a baking sheet. Using scissors, snip a cross on top of each ball. Cover and let rise until doubled in size, about 40 minutes.

◆ Preheat oven to 375°F.

◆ Mix the egg white with 1 tablespoon of water and brush the tops of the buns with the mixture.

◆ Bake until golden brown, about 20 minutes. Frost crosses on cooled buns with powdered sugar frosting.

Makes 24

Powdered sugar frosting

1 cup icing sugar

1 tbs lemon juice

1 tsp lemon zest

◆ Mix sugar with lemon juice and zest until smooth. Add a little water if needed, ½ teaspoon at a time.

◆ Place in a piping bag and pipe crosses on to buns in line with the crosses cut previously with scissors.

◆ Let dry before serving.

Pumpkin bread

½ cup unsalted butter or shortening

2 cups brown sugar

4 eggs

3 cups shredded uncooked pumpkin

⅔ cup water

3⅓ cups all-purpose flour

2 tsp baking soda

2 tsp baking powder

1 tsp salt

2 tsp cinnamon

1 tsp grated nutmeg

⅔ cup raisins

⅔ cup coarsely chopped nuts (optional)

½ cup toasted pumpkin seeds (optional)

◆ Preheat oven to 350°F. Grease bases only of 2 loaf pans, 9x5x3 inches.

◆ Beat the butter and sugar in a large mixing bowl until creamy. Add eggs one at a time and continue beating until mixture is light colored. Add the pumpkin and water, and blend.

◆ In a separate bowl mix the flour, baking soda, baking powder, salt and spices. Add to pumpkin mixture and mix only until just combined. Stir in raisins, nuts, if using, and half the pumpkin seeds, if using.

◆ Pour into the loaf pans and sprinkle with remaining pumpkin seeds.

◆ Bake until a wooden pick inserted into the center comes out clean, about 45–50 minutes.

◆ Cool slightly, and loosen sides of loaves from pans. Remove from pans and cool completely before slicing.

◆ To store, wrap and refrigerate no longer than 10 days, or freeze.

Makes 2 loaves

Sada roti

This is a Trinidadian version of Mexican tortillas or Indian chapatis.
They are just a bit thicker and can be enjoyed with many Indian dishes.

4 cups all-purpose flour

1 tsp salt

4 tsp baking powder

1 tsp butter

◆ Combine the flour with the salt and baking powder. Rub butter into the flour. Add enough water to make a firm dough.

◆ Turn dough onto a lightly floured table and knead until smooth for about 5 minutes.

◆ Divide dough into 4 pieces. Form each piece of dough into a smooth ball. Cover with a damp towel and let rest for 15 minutes.

◆ Heat a baking stone until hot.

◆ Roll out dough balls to about ½ inch thickness.

◆ Place on heated baking stone, and cook until small bubbles appear on dough. Turn over roti and continue to cook for about 4 minutes longer. Using pot holders or a towel pull the baking stone away from the fire toward you to expose the open flame or heat element. Push a roti onto the open flame and swiftly turn around so that the roti begins to balloon. Remove from heat and wrap in towels. Repeat for other rotis.

Makes 4

Coconut orange muffins

2 cups all-purpose flour

½ cup wholewheat flour

½ cup brown sugar

1 tsp cinnamon

1 tbs baking powder

¼ tsp baking soda

2 tbs butter

¼ cup finely grated fresh coconut

2 eggs

¼ cup evaporated milk

¾ cup orange juice

1 tbs orange zest

◆ Preheat oven to 375°F.

◆ Combine all the dry ingredients in a mixing bowl. Rub in butter until mixture resembles fine crumbs. Add coconut.

◆ In a separate bowl beat the eggs until fluffy. Beat in the evaporated milk, orange juice and zest.

◆ Add wet mixture to dry mixture and stir only until combined. Mixture should be lumpy.

◆ Spoon into greased muffin cups and bake for 20–25 minutes, until a wooden pick inserted into one of the muffins comes out clean.

Makes 12

Cornmeal muffins with red pepper

½ cup all-purpose flour

½ cup yellow cornmeal

2 tbs sugar

2 tsp baking powder

½ tsp salt

¼ cup chopped sweet red pepper

½ cup milk mixed with ½ tbs lime juice

2 tbs vegetable oil

1 egg

◆ Preheat oven to 400°F.

◆ Combine all the dry ingredients, and add the peppers.

◆ Combine the wet ingredients. Add wet to dry ingredients and stir just to combine.

◆ Spoon batter into prepared muffin tins and bake for 20 minutes until golden.

Makes 12

Breads . . .

Poppyseed waffles *with guava nutmeg syrup*

1½ cups flour

¼ cup wheat bran

1 tbs baking powder

1 tsp cinnamon

¼ tsp grated nutmeg

¼ cup poppyseeds

2 eggs, separated

1 cup milk

1 tsp vanilla

⅓ cup unsalted butter or shortening

◆ Combine all the dry ingredients in a bowl. In another bowl beat the egg yolks with the milk and vanilla.

◆ Melt fat and add to milk mixture.

◆ Beat egg whites to stiff peaks.

◆ Add milk mixture to dry ingredients, stir only until combined. Fold in beaten egg whites.

◆ Pour batter into heated waffle iron and bake until brown and crisp.

Makes 6

Guava nutmeg syrup

1 tbs good quality guava jam

½ cup fresh orange juice

1 tbs lemon juice

½ tsp aromatic bitters

¼ tsp grated nutmeg

¾ tsp cornstarch, diluted in 2 tsp water

◆ Melt the jam in a small saucepan. Add all the other ingredients except the cornstarch and stir to combine.

◆ Bring to the boil, thicken with cornstarch and cool.

Makes about 1 cup

Double chocolate orange muffins

juice of 1 orange

about 1 cup milk

½ tbs lime juice

zest of 1 orange

1 cup all-purpose flour

½ cup cocoa powder

1 tbs baking powder

½ tsp baking soda

pinch salt

½ tsp cinnamon

⅓ cup brown sugar

2 eggs

¼ cup vegetable oil

½ cup chocolate chips

◆ Preheat oven to 375°F.

◆ Pour orange juice into a measuring cup and add milk to bring it to 1 cup. Add lime juice and let sit for 15 minutes.

◆ Combine orange zest with flour, cocoa, baking powder, baking soda, salt, cinnamon and sugar.

◆ Beat the eggs, and add the oil and the milk mixture.

◆ Add flour mixture to egg mixture. Fold in chocolate chips.

◆ Spoon into prepared muffin cups and bake for 20 minutes.

Makes 12

Breads . . .

Fluffy West Indian golden pancakes
with sautéed bananas

1 cup milk

1 tbs lime juice

1½ cups all-purpose flour

1 tbs brown sugar

2 tsp baking powder

½ tsp baking soda

1 tsp cinnamon

¼ tsp salt

2 eggs

2 tbs melted butter

½ tsp vanilla

1 ripe banana, sliced

◆ Combine milk with lime juice and let stand for 15 minutes until thick and curdled.

◆ In a mixing bowl combine the flour, sugar, baking powder, baking soda, cinnamon and salt.

◆ In a separate bowl beat the eggs until light. Add the curdled milk, melted butter, vanilla and banana.

◆ Add the wet ingredients to the flour mixture and stir only until combined. Your batter should be lumpy.

◆ Heat a non-stick frying pan and grease with a small amount of butter.

◆ Spoon about ⅓ cup of batter onto hot frying pan and spread gently. When small bubbles appear on the topside and the edges look cooked then flip the pancake, cook for a short while longer and remove to a plate. Keep pancakes warm while you are cooking the remainder. Serve pancakes topped with sautéed bananas.

Makes 8

Sautéed bananas

½ cup fresh orange juice

¼ cup brown sugar

¼ tsp grated nutmeg

2 bananas, sliced

◆ Combine the orange juice, sugar and nutmeg in a small saucepan and cook until mixture is thick. Add bananas and cook for 30 seconds more.

Melt-in-your-mouth dinner rolls

These rolls are very present in most of the Caribbean islands.
They are served at dinner time or tea time.

4–4½ cups bread or all-purpose flour

1 tbs instant yeast

1 cup milk

⅓ cup sugar

⅓ cup butter or shortening

1 tsp salt

2 eggs

◆ In a large mixer bowl combine 2 cups flour and the yeast.

◆ In a saucepan heat the milk, sugar, butter and salt until warm (115°–120°F).

◆ Add milk mixture to flour mixture. Mix well, then add eggs. Beat mixture on low speed, constantly scraping the sides of the bowl. Beat for 3 minutes at high speed.

◆ Stir in as much of the remaining flour as you can mix in with a spoon.

◆ Turn out onto a lightly floured surface. Knead in enough of the remaining flour to make a moderately stiff dough that is smooth and elastic (about 6–8 minutes' kneading). Place in a lightly greased bowl and cover with plastic wrap.

◆ Let rise at room temperature until doubled in bulk, about 1 hour.

◆ Preheat oven to 400°F.

◆ Punch down dough and divide in half. Cover, and let rest for 10 minutes.

◆ Shape into desired rolls. Cover, and let rise until rolls are nearly doubled in size (about 30 minutes).

◆ Bake in preheated oven for 12–15 minutes or until done.

Cheese and pepper crescents

2 cups wholewheat flour

1 cup baker's bran

2½–3 cups baker's or all-purpose flour

¼ cup sugar

1 tsp salt

2 tbs instant yeast

2 cups milk

½ cup butter, melted

1 egg white, beaten

2 tbs poppyseeds

For the filling

3 tbs butter, softened

1½–2 cups grated Cheddar cheese

⅓ cup sliced olives

½ cup diced sweet red pepper

◆ Prepare the dough. In a large bowl combine the wholewheat flour, bran and 1 cup baker's or all-purpose flour. Add sugar, salt, and yeast.

◆ Warm milk to 115°–120°F. Add melted butter and combine.

◆ Add milk mixture to flour mixture and knead to a soft dough. Add as much of the remaining flour as you can to make a soft but pliable dough. Cover and let rise until doubled in volume, about 45 minutes.

◆ Divide dough into 3 equal portions. Make each portion into a ball, cover and let rest for 10 minutes.

◆ On a lightly floured surface roll one ball of dough into a 12 inch circle. Spread with 1 tablespoon butter, sprinkle with about ½ cup grated cheese, and a third of the olives and peppers. Cut circle into 12 wedges.

◆ To shape rolls, begin at the wide end of the wedge and roll toward the point. Place rolls point down, 2–3 inches apart, on a greased baking sheet. Brush with beaten egg white and sprinkle with poppyseeds. Repeat for other 2 rounds.

◆ Cover and let rise until doubled in volume, about 20 minutes.

◆ Preheat oven to 400°F.

◆ Bake crescents for 12–15 minutes until nicely browned.

Makes 36

Dhalpourie roti

These are Indian flatbreads filled with a dry split pea mixture. Really worth a try, they go great with any curry dish. Sometimes the curry meats and vegetables are folded into the rotis, for a marvellous treat and meal!

½ lb yellow split peas

½ tsp saffron or turmeric powder

3 cloves garlic

3 tsp ground roasted cumin (geera)

1 lb all-purpose flour

2 tsp baking powder

1 tsp salt

½ cup melted butter

◆ Place split peas into a pot. Cover with water, add saffron and garlic and bring to the boil. Lower heat and boil for about 15–20 minutes until peas are tender and cooked but not mushy. Drain in a colander and cool.

◆ Grind peas to a fine consistency using a food processor or food mill. Season peas with salt to taste and cumin.

◆ Combine flour with baking powder. Add 1 teaspoon salt and enough cool water to make a soft pliable dough. Cover and let rest for 30 minutes.

◆ Divide dough into 8 pieces. Form into smooth balls and cover. Leave for 20–30 minutes.

◆ Pat each piece of dough into a 3 inch circle. Cupping the dough in your hands, fill the cavity with the dhal, about 1½ tablespoons. Bring the sides of the dough together at the top and pinch together so that the filled dough becomes a smooth ball. Repeat.

◆ Heat a baking stone. Roll the roti loyas or filled roti dough into an 8 inch circle about ⅛–¼ inch thick.

◆ Place on heated baking stone. Cook until bubbles appear. Flip roti and brush with melted butter, turn again and brush with butter. Roti should balloon – at this point it is cooked. Remove and repeat until all the roti are cooked.

Makes 8

> To roast cumin (geera) pods: Place pods in a greaseless, heated frying pan. Toss them around until they begin to pop and crackle. The cumin will become aromatic and dark brown. Remove and grind.

Breads . . .

Roti selection: Sada roti (front, page 175), Dhalpourie roti (center), Paratha roti (back, page 184)

Paratha roti

4 cups flour

1 tbs butter, softened, plus ¼ cup melted butter

1 tsp salt

4 tsp baking powder

¼ cup vegetable oil plus more for brushing

◆ Combine the flour with the 1 tablespoon butter, salt and baking powder. Add enough water to knead to a soft dough, cover and leave to rest for 30 minutes.

◆ Divide dough into 10 pieces, and form each piece into a ball.

◆ Combine the melted butter with the oil.

◆ Roll out each piece of dough into a 6 inch round, and brush with oil mixture.

◆ Cut the dough into half from the middle of the top edge, leave a 1 inch uncut portion at the base. Starting from the top right hand side portion, roll the dough all the way to the bottom and up the left side. Your dough should resemble a cone. Tuck the end under, and then push the pointed part into the dough, flatten slightly and rest for a further 30 minutes.

◆ Roll each piece of prepared dough on a lightly floured surface into an 8 inch circle. Cook on a hot baking stone. Turn, brush with oil, turn again and brush with oil. Cook until it balloons, then remove. Repeat with the remaining rotis.

◆ Beat the roti with your hands or a wooden spatula to break and flake. Serve with any curried dishes.

Makes 10

Potato roti

3 cups all-purpose flour

3 tsp baking powder

1 tbs butter, softened, plus ¼ cup butter, melted

1 cup cool water

For the filling

½ lb potatoes, peeled

½ cup finely chopped chives

1 tsp salt

1 tsp freshly ground black pepper

2 cloves garlic, minced

1 tbs ground roasted cumin (geera)

½ tsp pepper sauce, or to taste

¼ cup chopped chadon beni (cilantro)

Breads . . .

◆ Combine the flour and baking powder. Add the tablespoon of butter and rub it into flour until it is combined. Add the water and knead to soft dough. Cover and let rest for 30 minutes.

◆ Meanwhile, boil the potatoes and mash to a smooth consistency. While still hot add the chives, salt, black pepper, garlic, cumin, pepper sauce and chadon beni. Mix well.

◆ Divide the dough into 6 equal pieces. Flatten one piece in the palm of your hand to about a 3 inch circle and cup the dough.

◆ Put about 3 tablespoons of the potato mixture in the center and fold the dough over to cover the potato, like forming a dinner roll. Repeat with remaining dough and allow to rest for 15 minutes.

◆ Heat your baking stone or tawa.

◆ On a lightly floured board gently roll the roti as thin as possible without bursting, about ¼ inch thickness.

◆ Place the roti on the hot tawa and when tiny bubbles appear on the surface, quickly turn over. Brush cooked side with melted butter and turn again, brushing the other side with butter, and pressing the edges to ensure even cooking.

◆ At this point your rotis should have many large bubbles and should be cooked. Do not allow to brown too much. Remove and repeat for other rotis. Wrap roti in clean tea towels to keep warm.

Makes 6

Island corn bread

1½ cups cornmeal

1½ cups all-purpose flour

1 tbs sugar

1 tsp salt

1 tbs baking powder

½ tsp baking soda

2 eggs

1¼ cups milk

4 tbs vegetable oil

½ cup chopped chives

1 cup grated cheese

◆ Preheat oven to 375°F.

◆ In a large bowl combine the cornmeal, flour, sugar, salt, baking powder and baking soda.

◆ Beat the eggs in a separate bowl, then add milk and 2 tablespoons oil. Stir wet ingredients into dry ingredients. Stir in chives and cheese.

◆ Pour remaining oil into a baking pan and place on top of your stove to heat the oil. Spoon batter into pan – it should sizzle. Bake in oven for 45 minutes until it is done and feels springy to the touch. Cool for 10 minutes before cutting.

sweet breads

Coconut bake

Bakes are Caribbean breads, usually shaped into a flat disk-like shape and baked. They are usually split open and served hot with fish salads, eggs or cheese. For a lighter bake omit the grated coconut and use water in place of the coconut milk. You may also use one third wholewheat flour and two thirds baker's flour.

1 cup coconut milk

4$\frac{1}{2}$ cups all-purpose flour or bread flour

2 tsp instant yeast

$\frac{3}{4}$ tsp salt

1 tbs brown sugar

$\frac{1}{4}$ cup butter or shortening

$\frac{1}{4}$ cup freshly grated coconut

◆ Warm coconut milk to about 120°F.

◆ Place flour, yeast, salt and brown sugar into a mixing bowl. Add butter and rub it into the flour until the mixture resembles fine crumbs. Add the grated coconut and mix. Pour in enough coconut milk to make a firm dough. If more liquid is needed add a little water.

◆ Turn dough out onto a floured surface and knead lightly until smooth. Divide dough into 2 pieces and roll each piece into an 8 inch circle. Prick with a fork and place onto baking sheets. Let rest for 20 minutes.

◆ Preheat oven to 400°F.

◆ Bake for 15–20 minutes.

Makes 2

Coconut bake

Fried bakes

These are delightful deep-fried breads. They balloon when cooked and are almost hollow inside. Really mouthwatering! Serve then for breakfast with eggs, or with fish salads.

4 cups all-purpose flour

1 tsp salt

4 tsp baking powder

1 tsp brown sugar

1 tbs shortening

vegetable oil for frying

◆ Combine the flour, salt, baking powder and sugar in a mixing bowl. Add the shortening and rub into flour until mixture resembles fine crumbs. Add just enough water to make a soft dough.

◆ Knead on a floured surface for about 5 minutes, then leave dough to rest for 30 minutes.

◆ Divide dough in half and divide each half into 12 pieces. Rest dough for another 5 minutes.

◆ Roll out each piece to about 3 inches in diameter.

◆ Heat vegetable oil in a deep frying pan and fry bakes in the hot oil, making sure that they are covered in the oil. Turn and fry until fully ballooned or puffed. Remove and drain. Serve hot.

Makes 24

Floats

A deep-fried yeasted bread. Floats are traditionally served with fried fish or shark.

4 cups flour

2 tsp instant yeast

1 tsp salt

1 tbs sugar

1 tbs shortening

vegetable oil for frying

◆ Combine the flour with the yeast, salt and sugar. Rub in shortening until mixture resembles fine crumbs, then add enough warm water to make a soft dough.

◆ Knead for 5 minutes, form into a smooth ball, cover and rest for 30 minutes until doubled in size.

◆ Form dough into 8 balls. Let rise again for 15 minutes.

◆ Flatten balls into 4 inch rounds.

◆ Heat oil in a deep skillet and deep fry floats until they actually float to the top of the oil. Turn and fry until golden. Drain and serve hot.

Makes 8

Cornmeal bake with roasted red pepper and chives

1 cup cornmeal

1½ cups all-purpose flour

2 tsp instant yeast

½ tsp salt

1 tbs brown sugar

⅓ cup softened butter

1 roasted red pepper, seeded and chopped

⅓ cup chopped chives

1 cup warm water (approx 115°–120°F)

◆ Combine all the dry ingredients in a mixing bowl. Add butter and rub into flour until mixture resembles fine crumbs. Stir in the pepper and chives. Add water and knead to a firm dough.

◆ Roll into an 8 inch circle and prick with a fork. Place on a baking stone, cover, and let rise for 20 minutes.

◆ Preheat oven to 400°F.

◆ Bake for 20–30 minutes until cooked through.

Small and hot flavors

Caribbean cooking is synonymous with hot peppers. All through the islands, pepper sauces, chutneys and spicy and hot salsas are used with any dish to add an infusion of heat. Almost addictive, many eating establishments, be it fine dining or fast food places, serve their own version of pepper sauces to their customers, alongside other staples like salt, pepper, ketchup and mustard.

It is not unusual when enjoying a meal in the Caribbean to stroll into one's backyard or garden, pick a pepper from one's own pepper tree and enjoy it in its raw state with the meal, seeds and all!

Mango salsa

This salsa is a winner with grilled steak, fish or chicken.

2 mangoes, half-ripe, preferably julie, finely chopped

1 clove garlic, minced

½ Congo pepper, seeded and finely chopped, more or less to taste

1 tbs fresh lime juice

salt and freshly ground black pepper

¼ cup finely chopped coriander or chadon beni (cilantro)

◆ Combine mangoes, garlic, Congo pepper, lime juice, salt and pepper.

◆ Let stand for 1 hour before serving. Add the fresh coriander just before serving.

Makes about 3 cups

Spicy tomato salsa

6 large ripe tomatoes, peeled

1 tsp minced garlic

2 tbs fresh lime juice

1 tbs olive oil

½ Congo pepper, seeded and chopped

½ cup finely chopped chives

1 tsp chili powder

salt and freshly ground black pepper

2 tbs finely chopped chadon beni (cilantro)

◆ Chop tomatoes and combine with garlic, lime juice, olive oil, Congo pepper, chives, chili powder, salt and pepper. Taste and adjust seasonings.

◆ Before serving add chadon beni and stir.

◆ Serve with corn chips, grilled chicken or fish, or with your favorite Mexican dish.

Makes about 2 cups

Sweet pepper salsa

Sweet peppers are the same as bell peppers in the Caribbean. They are often referred to as sweet peppers to differentiate them from hot peppers.

1 cup diced sweet green pepper

1 cup diced sweet red pepper

½ Congo pepper, seeded and finely chopped, more or less to taste

¼ cup finely chopped chives

2 cloves garlic, finely minced

2 tomatoes, seeded and chopped

2 tbs olive oil

4 tsp fresh lime juice

¼ cup chopped coriander

◆ Combine green and red peppers, hot pepper, chives, garlic, tomatoes, oil and lime juice. Cover and refrigerate for 1–6 hours.

◆ Season with salt and freshly ground black pepper, mix in fresh coriander and serve.

◆ This salsa is ideal with grilled chicken breast, steak and roast beef.

Makes about 4 cups

Avocado and tomato salsa

This is similar to guacamole, except the addition of tomatoes and onion gives it a zesty taste!

2 avocados, peeled and chopped

4 tomatoes, peeled, seeded and chopped

1 small onion, preferably red onion, finely chopped

1 tsp minced garlic

1 hot pepper, seeded and chopped, or to taste

1 tbs lime juice

salt and freshly ground black pepper

⅓ cup finely chopped chadon beni (cilantro) or coriander

◆ Combine all the ingredients except the fresh herbs, until well blended, taking care not to crush the avocado. Add herbs just before serving. Taste and adjust seasonings.

Serves 4–6

and hot

Tamarind-mint chutney

2 cups peeled, ripe tamarind pods

2 tbs salt

2 cups granulated sugar

2 tbs ground roasted cumin (geera)

1/2 hot pepper, seeded and minced, more or less to taste

6 cloves garlic, minced

4 tbs chopped mint

◆ Put tamarind pods in a small saucepan and barely cover with boiling water. Let steep for 30 minutes.

◆ Remove the seeds from the tamarind and discard (a potato crusher works well to separate the seeds from the pulp). Add the salt, sugar, cumin, pepper and garlic, and stir to mix. Bring the mixture to the boil and remove from heat.

◆ Cool, and stir in the mint. Taste and adjust seasonings. The chutney should be slightly sour-sweet in taste.

Makes about 2 cups

Mango chutney

4 green mangoes, preferably mango rose

2 cloves garlic, minced

1/2 tsp sugar

1/2 tsp salt

1/2 tsp pepper sauce, or to taste

1/4 cup chopped chadon beni (cilantro)

◆ Peel mangoes and slice flesh. Place in a food processor with the rest of the ingredients. Process until minced.

◆ Taste and adjust seasoning.

Makes about 1 cup

Zesty barbecue sauce

1 tbs vegetable oil

1 onion, grated or minced

3 cloves garlic, minced

1 cup tomato ketchup

¼ cup brown sugar

2 tbs yellow mustard

2 tbs Worcestershire sauce

1 tsp hot pepper sauce

1 tbs dark rum (optional)

◆ Heat the oil in a small saucepan. Add the onion and garlic and sauté until fragrant. Add all the other ingredients and cook until mixture begins to boil. Remove from heat and cool.

Makes about 3 cups

Barbecue sauce with cumin and chili

1 cup tomato ketchup

⅓ cup brown sugar

½ cup Chinese chili sauce

½ cup red wine vinegar

2 tbs yellow mustard

1 tbs Worcestershire sauce

2 cloves garlic, minced

1 tbs vegetable oil

2 tsp ground cumin (geera)

◆ Combine all the ingredients in a saucepan. Bring to the boil, remove from heat and cool before using.

Makes about 2 cups

Mandarin or portugal vinaigrette

Portugals are very large mandarins found in the Caribbean. They are just as delicious as mandarins but tend to have a stronger pulp.

¼ cup olive or sunflower oil

1 tbs red wine vinegar

2 tbs portugal juice or mandarin juice

1 clove garlic, minced

½ tsp freshly ground black pepper

½ tsp ground cumin (geera)

salt

◆ Whisk ingredients together until well blended. Chill and serve on your favorite salad greens and citrus fruits.

Makes ½ cup

Herbed vinaigrette dressing

2 tbs vinegar (red wine, herb or cider) or 2 tbs lemon juice

pinch sugar

salt and freshly ground black pepper

2 cloves garlic, minced

1 tsp Dijon mustard

6 tbs olive oil

2 tbs finely chopped fresh herbs (parsley, mint, basil or chives)

◆ Process the vinegar or lemon juice with the sugar, salt, pepper, garlic and mustard in a blender or food processor.

◆ Pour the oil in a thin stream and blend continuously until a thick emulsion is formed.

◆ Pour into a small bowl and stir in the fresh herbs. Let stand for a while until ready to use.

Makes about ½ cup

Small . . .

Glossary

An index of Caribbean indigenous ingredients and possible substitutions.

Accra A fritter made from salted cod, usually enjoyed at breakfast time.

Allspice Also called Jamaican pimento, this is the dried berry of the pimento tree and resembles a smooth and large black peppercorn. It is a main ingredient in Jamaican jerk marinade, and is also used in pickling meats.

Aloo Hindi for potato.

Amchar A hot and spicy-tasting mango pickle, usually made from dried and shredded mangoes flavored with pepper, curry massala and mustard oil. Also called anchar.

Arepas A Venezuelan-inspired dish, these are little fried cornmeal pastries stuffed with a spicy meat filling.

Avocado A pear-shaped fruit with a thick green skin which encloses a creamy yellow flavorful pulp. Delicious in soups, salads and salsas.

Bake A flat rounded bread that is either fried or baked.

Banana leaves The green leaves of the banana tree. They are usually used as a wrapping for foods to be steamed. They impart a delicate flavor to foods.

Bodi A Trinidadian name for a bean much like a green bean but more than a foot long.

Boucanee The name given to slow smoking of meat using fire, certain types of wood and wet leaves.

Breadfruit A round green starchy fruit on the outside, very fleshy with a pale yellow to white flesh. It is cooked and eaten as a side dish, but can be used in a variety of ways – sautéed, French fried, souffléd, grilled. It's also used in savory pies and in breads.

Bull jhol, also called Buljol A French-derived name for a salad usually made with salted cod, fresh tomatoes, boiled eggs, onions, peppers and avocado. Usually served in Trinidad at brunch or breakfast. May also be made with smoked herring.

Buss up shut The colloquial name given to paratha roti, or flaky type bread. The name derives from 'burst-up shirt' due to the torn or ragged appearance of the bread.

Calabaza The name given to West Indian pumpkin. This type is much denser than many, with a lower water content, hence being much more delicious. It is also known as crapaud back pumpkin, a name reflecting its characteristic knobbly skin.

Callaloo A name given to the characteristic leaf of the dasheen/taro plant. It is the main ingredient in a soup with the same name, which is seasoned or cooked with ochroes, coconut milk and crab. Spinach is a suitable substitute.

Carailli A knobbly-textured green vegetable more commonly referred to as bitter melon. It can be either cooked and enjoyed as a vegetable or eaten raw in pickles. The bitterness can be lessened by sprinkling slices with salt, leaving for about 30 minutes, then squeezing and rinsing.

Carite A type of fresh fish resembling snapper in taste and texture.

Cassareep Boiled down cassava juice used in Guyanese pepperpot soups/stews.

Cassava An edible root vegetable from the cassava root. Also known as yuca, it is usually boiled and prepared as a vegetable.

Chadon beni See cilantro.

Channa Also known as chickpeas or garbanzo beans.

Chives West Indian chives tend to be a lot fatter and have a stronger flavor than the finer variety. Both the green and white portions are used in cooking – they are often puréed to a fine paste and added to marinades for meat and seafood.

Christophene Also known as chayote, this resembles summer squash with a rigid green skin and a pale translucent flesh. It is used as a vegetable in stirfries, mixed vegetables and au gratin style. It can also be boiled and stuffed.

Chutney A very spicy condiment brought to the Caribbean by the East Indians, it is usually made with grated green mangoes or tamarind and seasoned with fresh hot peppers, cilantro and spices.

Cilantro/culantro A South American herb with the same flavor as Chinese parsley. Also known as chadon beni (shadow beni) in Trinidad.

Coconut jelly The soft white jelly that clings to the inside of a young coconut. It can be eaten straight from the open coconut shell, once the water is removed

Coconut water Water from the young coconut.

Congo pepper A hot pepper species in Trinidad, also called scotchbonnet pepper in Jamaica and habanero in Mexico.

Coo-coo A cornmeal dish much like polenta, the Trinidadian dish is made with cornmeal, ochroes and coconut milk. The Bajan version omits the coconut milk.

Cushcush A type of West Indian yam.

Dasheen A large root tuber whose young leaves are used as the main ingredient in callaloo. It is very starchy and can be either purplish or white.

Dhal An East Indian soup made with yellow or green split peas and seasoned with cumin, garlic, saffron and pepper.

Doubles Street food in Trinidad, this is curried channa served between two pieces of yeasted fried bara bread. Served with chutneys.

Eddo A root vegetable, somewhat slimy in texture, can be white or purplish in color. Very common in the Caribbean, ordinary potato may be used instead. It is related to the dasheen tuber, which is much larger and starchier in texture.

Figs Finger bananas.

Flan A baked custard, very similar to crème caramel. All islands have their own version of it.

Foo-foo Mashed and boiled green plantains, seasoned to taste.

Geera Cumin.

Ginger beer A delicious drink made traditionally at Christmas time in Trinidad and Tobago. Made from grated raw ginger that is steeped in water with cloves and other spices, it is then strained and sweetened. Very strong with a good ginger flavor.

Granadilla Same as passion fruit.

Ground provisions A collective name for root vegetables, such as yams, cassavas, tannia, eddoes, dasheen, etc.

Hops bread Name given to a crusty light large-size roll, originating from Trinidad.

Jerk Jamaican seasoning. Also a method of cooking meat that originates from Jamaica.

Kurma A Trinidadian East Indian sweet. A flour mixture is fried to a light crisp and dipped in a sugar solution.

Kutchela A hot and spicy East Indian condiment made from dried shredded green mango and seasoned with garlic, massala, spices and mustard oil.

Massala A blend of spices used in curry dishes.

Mauby A drink made from steeping the bark of the mauby or Caribbean carob tree. It is sweetened and served very cold. Flavor resembles anise.

Melongene Aubergine or eggplant.

Mixed essence A variety of different essences, mixed together, bottled, and sold in supermarkets. The most common flavors are almond, vanilla and anise. This is used in West Indian sweet breads and some cakes.

Ochro Okra.

Oil-down Also known as oiled-down or run-down. A method of cooking root vegetables or breadfruit in coconut milk until the coconut milk is absorbed leaving behind some coconut oil at the base of the pan.

Passion fruit A highly perfumed fruit, with a thick hard inedible outer peel and a bright yellow pulp which adheres to tiny black seeds. Quite sour in taste, with a high perfumed flavor. Excellent to flavor sorbets, ice creams and juices.

Pastelle A popular Christmas dish in Trinidad consisting of a cornmeal dough stuffed with a spicy meat filling, wrapped in a banana leaf and steamed.

Paw paw An orange-fleshed fruit whose center is filled with tiny black seeds. Same as papaya.

Pelau A rice, peas and meat casserole dish flavored with coconut milk.

Phoulorie An East Indian inspired split pea fritter.

Pigeon peas A rounded pea similar to black eye.

Plantain A member of the banana family. Plantains are not edible until cooked. They can be cooked at any stage, from green when they are used in savory dishes, to very ripe when they are fried or made into desserts.

Ponche de crème Also called poncha crème, a traditional Christmas drink made in Trinidad and Tobago, similar to egg nog.

Provisions These boil very much the same way as English potatoes. Simply peel your provisions, cut them into large chunks, 3 inch pieces, cover with lots of fresh water, add salt and boil for 20–30 minutes until tender. Drain and serve.

Roti Much like a flour tortilla, but flavored with split peas or potato, this is used as the wrapping for curried vegetables or meat. The actual roti and its filling is also known as a roti.

Roukou Achiote or annato seeds, usually made into a red substance used to color foods while being cooked.

Run-down See oil-down.

Saheena An East Indian inspired fritter made with ground split peas and dasheen or spinach leaves.

Saltfish Also called salt cod, a very salty dried fish that must be soaked in water and rinsed several times before using.

Sancoche A hearty soup made with ground provisions (root vegetables) and dumplings.

Sewain Also called sawine, a sweet milky dessert made with toasted vermicelli and flavored with cardamom and cinnamon. It is eaten on the Muslim festival of Eid ul Fitr.

Shadow beni A Trinidadian nickname for chadon beni. Its Spanish counterpart is culantro; the Hindus call it bandhania, meaning false dhannia.

Sumac A Middle Eastern dried spice made from the dried berries of the *Rhus coriaria* plant. Once ground, this coarse-textured powder is almost dark maroon in color. It has a lemony flavor and is used in salads and other Lebanese dishes.

Talkaree An East Indian Trinidadian technique of cooking down vegetables as an accompaniment to rice or roti.

Tannia A starchy root vegetable.

Taro A root vegetable much like eddoes.

Tawa From the East Indian name tava, it is a large flat cast-iron griddle used to cook flatbreads like rotis and tortillas.

Toolum A sticky sweet candy made from using molasses and coconut.

Topi tambo A small oval tuber with a very fine light brown skin covered with fibrous hairs. It has the texture of a Chinese water chestnut but can be substituted for Jerusalem artichokes in recipes. West Indians enjoy topi tambo as a snack, boiled in salted water then peeled. It is also good in sautés and stirfries.

Tostones A Latin American /Caribbean dish consisting of mashed and fried half-ripe plantains.

Yam Another West Indian tuber, also called African yam, this is large, white and very starchy. Not at all like American yams, which are yellow and sweet.

Yuca Cassava.

Zaboca Avocado.

Index

Page numbers in *italics* refer to illustrations.